The FIBRE-PLAN COOKBOOK

The FIBRE-PLAN COOKBOOK

M Y R A S T R E E T

A QUINTET BOOK

Published by Apple Press Ltd
293 Gray's Inn Road
London WC1X 8QF

ISBN 0 85076 054 3

This book was designed and produced by
Quintet Publishing Limited
6 Blundell Street, London N7

Art Director Peter Bridgewater
Editor Nicholas Law
Photographer John Heseltine

Typeset in Great Britain by
Central Southern Typesetters Limited, Eastbourne
Colour origination in Hong Kong by
Universal Colour Scanning Limited, Hong Kong
Printed in Hong Kong by Leefung-Asco
Printers Limited

CONTENTS

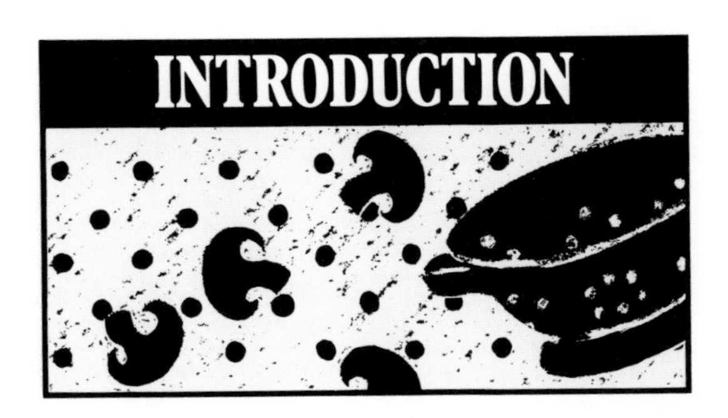
INTRODUCTION

There have been many dramatic developments in nutrition over the past few years and one of the most interesting and valuable pieces of research to emerge is the detrimental effect on Western diets when fiber is removed in the processing of the food we eat.

What is this fiber which sophisticated methods of food processing have been removing? In very simple terms, it is a mixture of complex polysaccharides in plant cell walls. However, dietary fiber is a complicated subject and much research is still being done. It is known that diseases of the bowel, constipation, appendicitis, hiatus hernias, piles and varicose veins are all very prevalent in developed society. Researchers have noted the comparatively low incidence of these afflictions in undeveloped countries, where much of the food eaten has little processing and the diet consists mainly of cereals, potatoes, root vegetables and legumes such as peas and beans.

Eating habits are unlikely to change overnight but it is well worth becoming familiar with foods that contain fiber and including them in everyday eating. At the same time, animal fats and refined sweet foods, which are such a major part of our diet, should be reduced. Fortunately many more people are becoming interested in whole foods and healthy eating. A balanced diet is still an essential part of health and fitness and I think it is possible to eat well and maintain a healthy body through giving some consideration to the food eaten without going to extremes and being unfairly dubbed a food freak.

FOODS TO INCLUDE IN YOUR FIBER PLAN

The following foods contain fiber and are easily included in everyday cooking and eating. Familiarize yourself with the amount of fiber in each food and increase high-fiber foods gradually over a week, as a sudden concentrated dose may prove rather indigestible. The body adjusts best if these foods are introduced gradually.

CEREALS

White flour has only 70 per cent of the grain left after the milling process, whereas wholewheat flour can contain 100 per cent of the grain after the husk has been removed. Flour is made into bread which plays an important part in all our meals. Therefore just eating more bread is an excellent way to increase daily fiber intake. All bread contains fiber but the wholewheat variety has three times as much as white bread and is much more effective in helping with bowel disorders. This does not mean that white bread is bad for you; it is an excellent source of high-energy food and much more nutritious than fried foods or sticky cakes, but wholewheat bread is nonetheless a more convenient way to help the fiber plan. Brown rice, millet, corn, barley and rye are other cereals that contain fiber.

Bran is the outer layer of the wheat grain and is removed in the flour milling process. 15 g/½ oz will provide 7 g of fiber (about 2 level tbsp). Using bran is an excellent way to add fiber to other foods, for example muesli, granola and breakfast cereals, home-made bread and scones, and I find it an excellent coating for fish, chicken, meat and croquettes.

BREAKFAST CEREALS

There are now numerous breakfast foods made from the cereals mentioned above. Many have a fairly high fiber content but do check the side of the packet. Most cereals with bran in the name are sure to produce some contribution to the fiber plan. Weight watchers may like to eat cereal with skimmed (skim) milk. Try to avoid the sugar-coated varieties of breakfast cereals. However, if members of your family will not change, try adding some millers' bran.

Muesli has now become one of the most popular breakfast foods. There are many excellent commercially prepared varieties but again try to avoid the very sweet ones with added sugar or honey. Muesli is both cheap and simple to make at home.

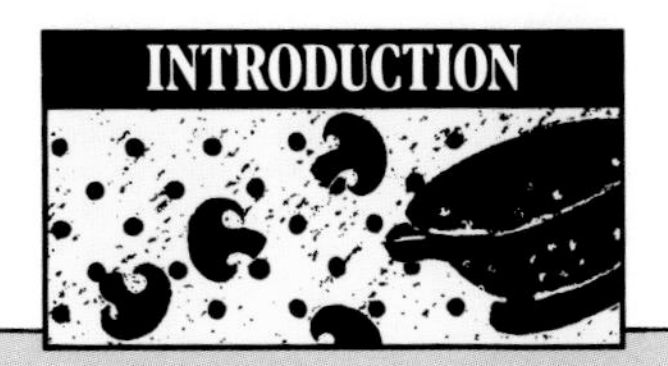

VEGETABLES, LEGUMES AND PULSES

This includes the bean family as well as peas and lentils. There are a vast array of different beans available and they make excellent additions to stews, soups, casseroles, salads and hot vegetable dishes. The ever-popular can of baked beans is an excellent, quick, easy source of adding fiber to a meal.

Frozen peas are a favourite vegetable and, when eaten often, can help the intake of fiber. Root vegetables are also helpful for increasing fiber. The average person consumes quite a few potatoes over a week. To add more fiber include parsnips, turnips, celery and aubergines (eggplant). Try not to add fat or butter to the root vegetables when you cook them. Potatoes are best cooked with their skins on and baked potatoes are excellent.

Salad vegetables have little fiber but are enjoyable to eat. As it is in any case a good idea to eat raw vegetables regularly, add grated carrot, cabbage, celery, mushrooms, cauliflower, watercress, potatoes and beans to your usual salad vegetables.

PULSES (LEGUMES)

This covers dried seeds such as peas, beans and lentils. These seeds are relatively inexpensive and have a high protein and fiber content. They are, therefore, a valuable addition to a whole foods or vegetarian diet, where meat and fish may be excluded.

To prepare

♦ Pick out any black or discoloured seeds and discard them. Wash the remaining seeds under running water unless the packet states that the seeds are pre-washed.

♦ Place green or yellow peas, chick peas (garbanzos), beans, haricot (navy), butter (lima), red kidney, aduki (azuki), etc, in a basin and cover with cold water. Steep overnight before cooking.

Lentils do not need to be soaked.

It is not, as some people think, just bran, cereal and wholewheat bread that are high in fiber. Other fiber-rich foods are peas, various beans, lentils, nuts and dried fruits, all of which can be used to make very tasty and varied dishes. Another misconception about fiber-rich foods is that they are fattening; this need not be so. Indeed, high-fiber diets have proved both popular and successful for some slimmers. The advantage of eating high-fiber foods is that they leave less room for the high-calorie snacks and sweet foods, which are so tempting to satisfy between-meal hunger. In fact, research has shown that it is possible for fiber to act as a buffer against consuming high-energy foods, because hunger pangs are reduced. It can also help the digestion and absorption of other energy foods.

The daily quantity of fiber recommended for keeping the body in good running order is only 40 g (just over 1½ oz). There is no need to eat your daily quota of high fiber in one, large unpalatable bowl of bran. Instead, you can introduce greater quantities of fiber to your favourite daily recipes. For instance, a little less meat (animal fat) and a little more root vegetable with, perhaps, some beans, will not be noticed in a casserole if the flavour is still good.

I hope that the information on fiber and the selection of recipes will enable you to enjoy extra fiber in your diet. Also, greater awareness of the value of fiber in everyday dishes may help prevent unpleasant illness in your family as well as contributing to their general fitness.

To cook

♦ Drain the pulses (legumes), cover with plenty of cold water. *Note* Salt should not be added at this stage – while the pulses (legumes) remain hard.

♦ Bring to the boil and simmer gently until soft. The cooking time will vary according to the age of the seeds and can be anything from 15 minutes to nearly 1½ hours, so it is essential to test as the cooking proceeds.

♦ As the seeds become tender, add 1 tsp salt for each 1 cup/250 g/8 oz and simmer for a further 10 to 15 minutes.

The cooking liquid can be used for making soups and adding to stews.

Special note

It is essential to boil red kidney beans for at least 45 minutes before using in salads or any dish that does not require a long cooking time.

GRAINS

Long-grain brown rice is ordinary long-grain rice that has been milled only to remove the inedible husk. It contains fiber and valuable B vitamins, some minerals and a small amount of protein.

Brown rice has a distinct nutty flavour and is less fluffy when cooked. It has a slightly chewy texture in the mouth, looks very similar to any other long grain rice but is a soft brown colour. Sometimes brown rice gives off a peculiar smell when cooking. There are now several easy cook varieties available, and these usually have specific cooking instructions on the packet.

BOILED LONG-GRAIN BROWN RICE

Ingredients

1 cup/250 g/8 oz long-grain brown rice

2½ cups/600 ml/1 pt water

½ teaspoon salt

To prepare

♦ Wash the rice well under the cold tap unless it is pre-washed. Drain.

♦ Bring the water to the boil and sprinkle in the rice and the salt. Fork through to separate the grains, bring water back to the boil for about 1 minute. Then cover the pan and turn the heat to very low. After simmering for about 20 minutes, test a few grains. All the water should be absorbed; however, if the rice is not cooked, add 2 tbsp cold water and continue cooking for a further 3–5 minutes.

Note

Brown rice usually takes longer than white rice to cook, but there are now quick-cook varieties on the market which will require only about 15 minutes. Some varieties from health food stores can take as long as 50 minutes to cook and will need four measures of water to one of rice.

Serves 4

NUTS

This high-protein food is rich in the B vitamins and has a good fiber content. Nuts are a valuable addition to everyday meals and can be introduced into meat and vegetable dishes as well as salads and baked goods.

DRIED FRUITS

Useful sources of fiber are apricots, prunes, figs, sultanas (white raisins), currants and raisins. Use dried fruit salads for breakfast and desserts. Cakes, biscuits or cookies are much more filling if made with dried fruit and nuts. Dried fruit can also be added to breakfast cereals and muesli.

Bread and Cereal products	g fiber per 100 g/3½ oz
Wholewheat bread	8.5
Brown bread	5.1
Hovis (wheat germ)	4.6
White bread	2.7
Wholewheat flour (100 per cent)	9.6
Brown flour (85 per cent)	7.5
White flour (72 per cent) (for breadmaking)	3.0
Household flour, plain (all purpose)	3.4
Self-raising flour	3.7

Biscuits and Crackers	g fiber per 100 g/3½ oz
Rye crispbread (wafers)	11.7
Plain digestive (Graham wafers)	5.5
Bran wheat	44.0
Oatmeal, raw	7.0
Pearl barley, raw	6.5

Breakfast Cereals	g fiber per 100 g/3½ oz
All Bran	26.7
Cornflakes	11.0
Grapenuts	7.0
Muesli	7.4
Puffed wheat	15.4
Ready Brek	7.6
Rice Krispies	4.5
Shredded Wheat	12.3
Special K	5.5
Sugar Puffs	6.1
Weetabix	12.7

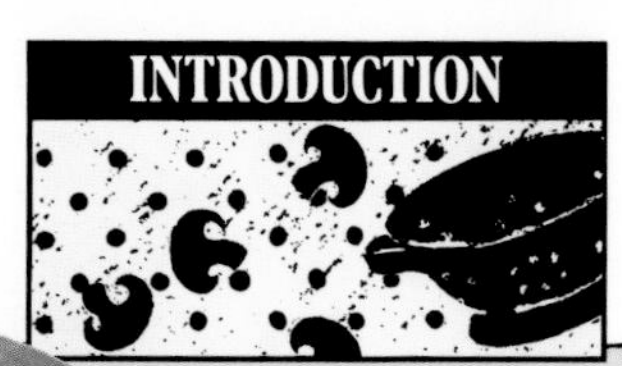

Fresh Vegetables	g fiber per 100 g/3½ oz
Aubergine (eggplant), raw	2.5
Broccoli tops, raw	3.6
Cabbage, white, raw	2.7
Cabbage, red, raw	3.4
Carrots, raw	2.9
Carrots, boiled	3.1
Cauliflower, raw	2.1
Cauliflower, boiled	1.8
Celery, raw	1.8
Celeriac, raw	4.9
Cucumber, raw	0.4
Gourd, bitter, raw, fresh	4.0
Leeks, raw	3.1
Leeks, boiled	3.9
Lettuce, raw	1.5
Mushroom, raw	2.5
Olives in brine	4.4
Parsley, raw	9.1
Parsnip, raw	4.0
Parsnip, boiled	2.5
Pepper, raw and boiled	0.9
Potato, raw	2.1
Potato, baked, flesh only	2.5
Radishes, raw	1.0
Spring onion (scallion), flesh of bulb	3.1
Sweetcorn (corn), on the cob, kernels only, raw	3.7
Sweetcorn, canned, kernels only	5.7
Tomato, raw	1.5
Tomato, canned	0.9
Turnip, raw	2.8
Watercress, raw	3.3

Fruit – fresh and dried	g fiber per 100 g/3½ oz
Apples, eating, with skin and core	1.5
Apples, eating, flesh only	2.0
Apples, cooking, raw, flesh only	2.4
Apricots, dried, raw	24.0
Banana, raw	3.4
Blackberries, raw	7.3
Blackcurrants, raw	8.7
Breadfruit, canned, drained	2.8
Currants, raw	6.5
Dates, dried, raw	8.7
Figs, fresh, raw	2.5
Figs, dried	18.5
Guava, canned, whole	3.6
Loganberries, raw	6.2
Medlars, raw	10.2
Passion fruit, raw	15.9
Peaches, dried, raw	14.3
Pears, eating, flesh only	2.3
Pears, eating, with skin and core	1.7
Prunes, raw, with stones	13.4
Prunes, raw, no stones	16.1
Quinces, raw	6.4
Raisins, stoned, raw	6.8
Redcurrants, raw	8.2
Sultanas (white raisins), raw	7.0
Whitecurrants, raw	6.8

Legumes (pulses)	g fiber per 100 g/3½ oz
Butter (lima) beans, raw	21.6
Butter (lima) beans, boiled	5.1
Chickpeas (garbanzos), raw	15.0
Haricot (navy) beans, raw	25.4
Haricot (navy) beans, boiled	7.4
Kidney beans, raw	25.0
Lentils, red, raw	11.7
Mung beans, raw	22.0
Mung beans, canned	3.0
Papri beans, fresh, raw	6.3
Papri beans, canned, drained	4.6
Peanuts, fresh	8.1
Peas, fresh, raw	5.3
Peas, frozen, boiled	12.0
Pigeon peas, raw	15.0
Soya flour, full fat	11.9
Soya flour, low fat	14.8

Nuts	g fiber per 100 g/3½ oz
Almonds/badam	14.3
Barcelona nuts	10.3
Brazil nuts	9.0
Chestnuts	6.8
Cob or hazel nuts	6.1
Coconut, kernel only	13.6
Coconut, desiccated (shredded)	23.5
Peanuts, fresh	8.1
Peanuts, roasted and salted	8.1
Walnuts	5.2

Pasta and Rice	g fiber per 100 g/3½ oz
Brown rice, raw	4.2
Macaroni, raw	5.5
Noodles, wheat dried, raw	5.7
Spaghetti, raw	5.6
Wholewheat pasta, uncooked	10.0

Imaginative cooks can always produce delicious soups, and with the whole range of root and other vegetables as well as dried beans, lentils and barley to choose from, soups are a must. It is interesting to see that many of the old fashioned soups such as cock-a-leekie and lentil are high in fiber. There is nothing more nourishing and comforting on a cold day than a steaming bowl of soup with fresh brown bread. Cream soups are easily made in a blender or food processor and chilled soups are delicious starters

Use a good basic stock, well-flavoured with root vegetables, if you are making your own, but if using stock (bouillon) cubes remember that they tend to be salty so adjust the seasoning. Savoury dips with nuts are popular and can be served with raw vegetables or crudities. Try lemon juice or yoghurt dressings in place of those made with oil for favourite appetizers like avocados and prawns. Triangles or strips of wholewheat toast are ideal with creamy textured dishes.

COCK-A-LEEKIE SOUP

Ingredients
1 large chicken joint (piece) or 1 chicken carcase
1 onion, peeled
1 bay leaf
1 bouquet garni
salt and freshly ground pepper
4½ cups/1 litre/1¾ pt water
2 tbsp/25 g/1 oz brown rice
⅔ cup/100 g/4 oz prunes, soaked in water
450 g/1 lb leeks, washed
1 tbsp chopped parsley

To prepare

♦ Place the chicken joint or cooked carcase with the quartered onion in a saucepan. Add the bay leaf and bouquet garni with a sprinkling of seasoning. Pour on the water and bring to the boil. Simmer for 1 hour.

♦ Strain into a bowl, remove the chicken joint and chop into small pieces. If using a carcase, remove any meat left and leave aside.

♦ Skim any fat from the stock and return to the saucepan. Make up to 5 cups/2 pints with water or more chicken stock.

♦ Sprinkle in the brown rice, bring to the boil and simmer until the rice is almost cooked, approximately 20 minutes. Add the prunes and continue cooking for 5 minutes.

♦ Make a cross through the centre of each leek, having first removed any discoloured outside leaves. Wash thoroughly under a running tap. Chop into slices about ¾ cm/¼ in thick. Add to the soup. Cook on a simmering heat for a further 10–15 minutes.

♦ Lastly, stir in the cooked chicken. Serve piping hot garnished with parsley.

The addition of wholewheat bread makes an excellent snack meal.

Note

Chicken giblets can be added to the stock for extra flavour.

Serves 4

CORN CHOWDER

Ingredients

4 slices streaky bacon
1 medium onion, peeled and diced
1 potato, peeled and cubed
1½ cups/325 g/12 oz can corn kernels or frozen corn
2½ cups/600 ml/1 pt chicken stock
salt and freshly ground pepper
1¼ cups/300 ml/½ pt milk
¼ tsp Tabasco sauce
1 tbsp chopped parsley

To prepare

♦ Remove any rind from the bacon slices and cut into small pieces.

♦ On a low heat, place the bacon in a saucepan and allow to cook in its own fat. When there is a little fat in the pan, turn up the heat and allow to crisp. Add the onion and fry for 1 minute.

♦ Add the potato cubes, stir round, then add half the corn with the chicken stock and seasoning. Bring to the boil and simmer for 30 minutes. Allow to cool slightly and liquidize the soup in a blender or food processor.

♦ Return to the saucepan and stir in the milk and the remaining corn. Heat through over a low heat. Add Tabasco sauce and taste for seasoning.

♦ Sprinkle with chopped parsley.

Note

If preferred, the soup does not need to be liquidized. For this method, add milk gradually at the end of cooking time.

Serves 4

GREEN PEA AND LETTUCE SOUP

Ingredients
3¾ cups/900 ml/1½ pt chicken stock or water
1 large potato, peeled
1 cup/225 g/8 oz frozen peas
2 spring onions (scallions) or 1 small onion, peeled
1 bay leaf
1 bouquet garni
1 sprig parsley
salt and freshly ground pepper
1 lettuce, washed
To garnish
1 tbsp single (cereal) cream
1 tsp chopped green spring onion (scallion)

To prepare

♦ Place the stock or water in a large saucepan. Chop the potato into slices and add to the liquid, bring to the boil and simmer for 15 minutes.

♦ Add the frozen peas and simmer for a further 5 minutes.

♦ Chop the spring onions or finely chop the onion if spring onions are not available. (If using spring onions, retain a few green slices for garnish.)

♦ Add the onions, bay leaf and bouquet garni and sprig of parsley with some seasoning.

♦ Gradually add the lettuce torn into strips and simmer for a further 10 minutes.

♦ Allow to cool slightly and liquidize in a blender or food processor or rub through a mouli-strainer.

♦ Taste for seasoning and reheat if serving hot. Garnish with a swirl of cream and a few chopped green spring onions.

Serves 4

Variation

Serve chilled with a little single cream added as a delicious, cold, summer soup.

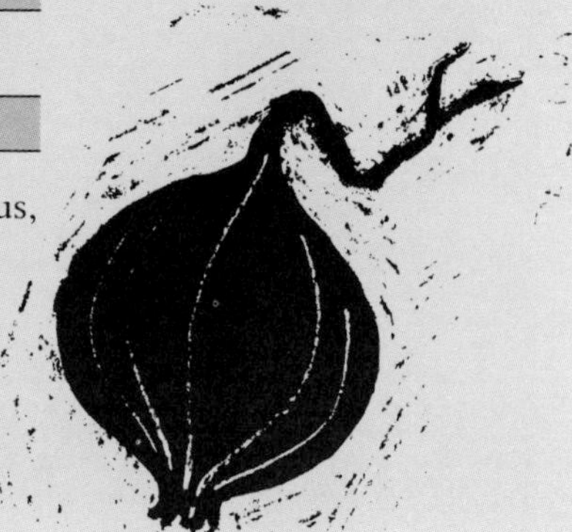

GREEN PEA SOUP

Ingredients

1 cup/225 g/8 oz dried peas (instructions below)
2 tbsp/25 g/1 oz butter
1 large onion, peeled
3¾ cups/900 ml/1½ pt stock or water
¼ tsp sugar
salt and freshly ground pepper
1 tsp chervil
1 bay leaf
1 bouquet garni
⅔ cup/150 ml/¼ pt milk
4 tbsp single (cereal) cream

To prepare

♦ Soak the dried peas in cold water overnight.

♦ Melt the butter in a large saucepan. Dice the onion and add to the butter, cook over a low heat for 4 minutes.

♦ Add the peas with 2½ cups/600 ml/1 pt stock or water, bring to the boil and simmer until cooked. (This will take about 35 minutes.) Allow to cool slightly.

♦ Liquidize the peas in a blender or food processor or pass through a mouli strainer. Return to the saucepan, add the sugar, seasoning and herbs.

♦ Over a low heat, add 1¼ cups/300 ml/½ pt stock and simmer for 10 minutes. Gradually add the milk and continue cooking on a low heat for a further 5 minutes. Remove the bouquet garni and bay leaf, taste for seasoning. Stir in the cream just before serving.

♦ Serve with slices of wholewheat bread, brown rolls or croûtons.

Serves 4

Variation

Use frozen peas for this recipe if preferred. Reduce cooking time in step 3 to 15 minutes.

FAMILY LENTIL SOUP

Ingredients
2 tbsp oil
1 large onion, peeled
1 carrot, scraped
2 sticks celery, washed
1 cup/250 g/8 oz red lentils, washed
1 sprig parsley
1 bay leaf
1 bouquet garni
salt and freshly ground pepper
5 cups/1¼ l/2 pt stock
To garnish
1 tbsp chopped parsley
wholewheat bread croûtons

To prepare

♦ Heat the oil over a low heat in a large saucepan.

♦ Dice the vegetables finely, add to the oil and allow to cook for 4 minutes.

♦ Add the washed lentils, parsley, bay leaf, bouquet garni, seasoning and stock. Bring to the boil and simmer gently for about 35 minutes, until the lentils are cooked. If necessary, skim the surface from time to time.

♦ Taste for seasoning and adjust. Serve with chopped parsley sprinkled on top and a dish of croûtons.

Serves 4

Variation

Cream of lentil soup can be made by liquidizing the soup and reheating slowly with 4 tbsp milk and 2 tbsp cream.

LENTIL AND TOMATO SOUP

Ingredients
½ cup/100 g/4 oz red lentils, washed
1 large onion, peeled
1 small turnip, peeled
1 parsnip, peeled
2 stalks, celery, washed
1½ cups/450-g/15-oz can tomatoes
4½ cups/1 l/1¾ pt stock or water
1 bay leaf
1 bouquet garni
salt and freshly ground pepper
To garnish
wholewheat croûtons
1 tbsp chopped parsley

To prepare

♦ Wash and rinse the lentils removing any discoloured or black pieces.

♦ Chop the vegetables roughly into even-sized pieces.

♦ Put the lentils, vegetables, tomatoes and stock or water into a large saucepan with the bay leaf and bouquet garni. Season well.

♦ Bring the soup to the boil and remove and skim. Lower the heat to allow liquid to simmer for about 35 minutes, until vegetables and lentils are tender. Allow to cool slightly.

♦ Liquidize the soup in a blender or food processor or rub through a mouli-strainer. If the mixture is too thick, add a little more stock, milk or water. Reheat and taste for seasoning.

♦ Serve with wholemeal bread croûtons and a sprinkling of chopped parsley.

CREAM OF MUSHROOM SOUP

Ingredients
6 cups/350 g/12 oz mushrooms
4 tbsp/2 oz/50 g butter
1 small onion, peeled
4½ cups/1 l/1¾ pt chicken stock
1 bouquet garni
1 bay leaf
2 tbsp white wine
1 tbsp wholewheat flour
salt and freshly ground pepper
To garnish
4 tbsp whipping cream
¼ tsp paprika
2 mushrooms, washed and sliced

To prepare

♦ Wash the mushrooms and retain two for garnish. Chop the remainder roughly.

♦ Heat half the butter in a large saucepan on a low heat.

♦ Chop the onion finely and add to the butter. Cook for 3 minutes. Add mushrooms and stir for a further 2 minutes.

♦ Add the stock, bouquet garni, bay leaf and white wine. Bring to the boil and simmer for 15 minutes. Allow to cool slightly.

♦ Liquidize the soup in a blender or food processor. If this is not possible, pass through a wide-meshed sieve or mouli-strainer.

♦ Heat the remaining butter in the cleaned saucepan, add the flour until a roux (a paste of flour and butter) is made. Cook for 1 minute, then gradually add the mushroom soup, stirring briskly. Season well.

♦ Add 2 tbsp cream just before serving.

♦ Mix the remaining cream with the paprika. Pour the soup into bowls and swirl the cream mixture on top. Decorate with a few slices of mushrooms.

Serve with fresh wholewheat bread.

Serves 4–6

SCOTCH BROTH

Ingredients
450 g/1 lb scrag neck of lamb
4½ cups/1 l/1¾ pt water
salt and freshly ground pepper
1 bay leaf
2–3 tbsp pearl barley
2 tbsp dried peas, soaked
2 carrots, scraped
1 large onion
1 small turnip, peeled
3 leeks, washed
1 tbsp chopped parsley

To prepare

♦ Place the trimmed meat into a large saucepan with the water, 1 tsp salt, pepper and the bay leaf. Add the pearl barley and peas. Bring to the boil and simmer for 1 hour. Remove the meat and cut into small pieces.

♦ Cut the carrots into dice, the onions into small dice and the turnip into slices and then small dice.

♦ Cut a cross down the leeks and wash thoroughly, then slice.

♦ Skim away any fat that has risen to the surface of the broth. Add the carrots, onions and turnips and bring back to the boil and skim. Simmer for a further 15–20 minutes. Then add the leeks and cook for a further 10 minutes with the meat.

♦ Skim any fat from the surface with kitchen paper (paper towels). Toss in the chopped parsley, and serve with slices of wholewheat bread.

As this soup is a meal in itself, it is ideal for a lunchtime snack.

Serves 4–6

DEVILS ON HORSEBACK

Ingredients
12 prunes, soaked
6 slices streaky bacon
12 cocktail sticks (tooth picks)

To prepare

♦ Place the soaked prunes in a small saucepan covered with water, bring to the boil and simmer for 5 minutes. Drain and allow to cool slightly.

♦ Remove the stones from the prunes and reshape.

♦ Cut the rind from the bacon, cut each slice in half and smooth out with a spatula. Place a piece of foil on the grill pan (broiler) and arrange the slices of bacon on the foil. Cook for 2 minutes under a hot grill (broiler). Do not allow to crisp.

♦ When slightly cooled, wrap the bacon pieces around the prunes and finish cooking under the grill (broiler) or in the oven if more convenient.

♦ Secure with cocktail sticks. Serve as an appetizer with pre-dinner drinks.

Makes 12

RED BEAN SOUP

Ingredients
1¾ cups/425-g/15-oz can kidney beans
1 tbsp oil
1 onion, peeled and diced
1 clove garlic, crushed
1 tsp oregano
¼ tsp chili powder
salt and freshly ground pepper
1½ cups/425-g/15-oz can tomatoes
2½ cups/600 ml/1 pt beef stock
2 tbsp chopped parsley

To prepare

♦ Drain the kidney beans and rinse under the tap.

♦ Heat the oil in a large saucepan and cook the onion over a low heat for 2 minutes. Add the garlic and cook for a further 1 minute.

♦ Add the kidney beans and mash slightly with a fork. Add all the remaining ingredients except the parsley. Bring to the boil, reduce the heat and simmer for 5 minutes.

♦ Stir well to break down the tomatoes and then continue cooking for 10 minutes. Taste for seasoning, add the parsley before serving with fresh wholewheat bread.

Serves 4

PISTOU SOUP

Ingredients
½ cup/100 g/4 oz butter (lima) beans, soaked
10 cups/2 l/4 pt water
2 carrots, scraped
1 small turnip, peeled
2 large potatoes, peeled
2 courgettes (zucchini)
2 large leeks, washed
2 cups/225 g/8 oz runner (large green) beans
2½ cups/600 ml/1 pt stock
⅓ cup/50 g/2 oz small wholewheat pasta
salt and freshly ground pepper
To season
2 cloves garlic, crushed
2 sprigs fresh basil
2 tomatoes, skinned
1 tbsp tomato purée (paste)
½ cup/50 g/2 oz Gruyère cheese, grated
3 tbsp olive oil

To prepare

♦ Cook the butter beans, which have been soaked overnight, for 10 minutes in a large saucepan with 10 cups/2 l/4 pt water.

♦ Cut the carrots and turnip into strips. Add to the beans after 10 minutes. Cut the potatoes into cubes and the courgettes into chunks, add to the soup.

♦ Cut the leeks in thick slices and runner beans into strips. Add a further 2½ cups/600 ml/1 pt stock, which can be made with a stock (bouillon) cube, to the soup. Stir in the leeks and the beans.

♦ Bring the mixture to the boil again and simmer for 1 hour, stirring from time to time to mash the larger pieces of vegetable.

♦ Add the pasta. Cook for 5 minutes, without stirring.

♦ Blend all the seasonings together in a blender or mash well in a bowl. Stir this mixture into the soup and stir gently until the pasta is cooked.

Note

Parsley can be used when basil is unobtainable.

Serves 4

CORN ON THE COB WITH OLIVE BUTTER

Ingredients
4 corn on the cob
¼ tsp sugar
4 tbsp/50 g/2 oz butter
1 spring onion (scallion), washed and sliced
12 green or stuffed olives
1 tbsp chopped parsley
2 tsp capers
salt and freshly ground pepper
1 tbsp lemon juice
½ tsp grated lemon rind

To prepare

♦ Remove the hairy husk and trim the stalk end of the corn. Cook in unsalted water with ¼ tsp sugar for 15 minutes. The cooking time will depend on the freshness of the corn – corn picked from a garden and cooked immediately may need only 5 minutes cooking time.

♦ Melt the butter on a very low heat, add the sliced spring onion and olives, allow to cook for 1 minute. Add the parsley, capers, seasoning, lemon juice and rind.

♦ Drain the corn and serve hot with the olive butter spooned on each.

Note

If using frozen corn, follow cooking instructions on the packet.

Serves 4

HOLLANDAISE SAUCE

Ingredients
¾ cup/150 g/6 oz butter
2 tbsp water
6 slightly crushed peppercorns
1 tbsp white wine vinegar
2 egg yolks
1 tbsp lemon juice
salt to taste

To prepare

♦ Make the sauce in a double boiler or heatproof bowl over a saucepan of hot water. If using the latter method, make sure that the bottom of the bowl is not touching the hot water or the sauce will set on the bottom of the bowl before it is cooked.

♦ Cut the butter into pieces and melt, without turning to oil, in a small saucepan.

♦ Place the water, crushed peppercorns and white vinegar in a small saucepan and reduce to about 1 tbsp liquid.

♦ Whisk the egg yolks, reduced liquid and a little of the butter in the double saucepan. When the mixture becomes creamy and slightly thick, pour in the butter in a thin stream, whisking briskly. Add lemon juice and a little salt, taste for seasoning.

♦ Remove from the heat immediately when it is thick. Should the sauce look as if it is curdling, it can usually be rescued by the addition of a few drops of cold water and a further brisk whisking.

Note

This sauce can be made in a liquidizer or food processor, but less butter may be absorbed and the addition of 1 tbsp cold water with the lemon juice will prevent it becoming too thick.

Makes 1¼ cups/300 ml/½ pt

ASPARAGUS WITH HOLLANDAISE SAUCE

Ingredients
700 g/1½ lb asparagus
1¼ cups/300 ml/½ pt Hollandaise sauce (see page 28)

To prepare

As this is usually a very expensive vegetable, it is important to cook it properly so that the stalks are cooked and the tips are not over-cooked. Few people have proper asparagus pans, where the vegetable can stand up to enable the tougher stalks to be cooked in the water and the tips by the steam, therefore improvisation is called for. Some people do cook the asparagus on its side in a large frying pan with the tips supported out of the water but great care has to be taken if using this method.

♦ Feel the stalks of the asparagus and, where the stem becomes woody, cut at this point. Try to keep the stems roughly the same length. Retain the stems and cook with the asparagus as this can be made into stock for soup.

♦ Tie the asparagus into four bunches and secure with twine or string. Prepare a piece of foil to fit around the edge of the saucepan, by crumpling.

♦ Pour 7.5 cm/3 in boiling water into a saucepan. Add 1 tsp salt and a few drops of lemon juice. Stand the bundles upright in the saucepan and wedge with the ring of crumpled foil. When they are suitably arranged, place a single layer of foil over the saucepan and the asparagus. Bring to the boil and cook briskly. The time required will depend on the thickness and freshness of the asparagus, but test after 12 minutes by making a slit in the foil and testing a spear with a small vegetable knife. If the tips seem to be tender, lift out a bundle with the string and test the stalks, which should have cooked in the water while the tips were cooked in the steam. Some thick asparagus may take 40 minutes to cook.

♦ Serve with Hollandaise sauce.

Serves 4

Variation

To make a mousseline sauce, add 4 tbsp whipped cream to the Hollandaise sauce as it cools. Serve cold with fish or vegetables.

CRUDITIES

Ingredients
1 green pepper, seeded
1 red pepper, seeded
4 stalks celery, washed
1 small cauliflower, washed
4 mushrooms, washed
2 medium carrots, scraped

To prepare

♦ Wash all the vegetables thoroughly as they are served raw.

♦ Cut the peppers into sticks roughly the same size. Drop into a bowl filled with iced water.

♦ Remove the strings from the celery with a potato peeler and cut into strips of similar size to the peppers. Place in the iced water.

♦ Divide the cauliflower into florets (floweretts) and trim away excess stalk. Add to the iced water.

♦ Cut the mushrooms in thick slices or, if small, leave whole. Add to the other vegetables.

♦ Cut the carrots into sticks approximately the same size as the peppers and celery.

♦ Drain the vegetables well and dry on kitchen paper (paper towels). Arrange in and serve with a dip.

Serves 4

Variations

Small (canned) artichoke hearts may be added.

Washed and prepared spring onions (scallions). If green tops are sliced down and the onions placed in iced water, they will curl to make an added decoration to the dish.

Small whole, washed tomatoes are often added.

A dish can be arranged with crudities on one side of the dips and pickled vegetables such as olives, gherkins and small onions on the other. Provide cocktail sticks (tooth picks) for guests to make a choice.

AUBERGINE (EGGPLANT) DIP

Ingredients

1 large aubergine (eggplant)

2 tbsp oil

1 clove garlic, crushed

⅔ cup/150 ml/¼ pt yoghurt

juice of half lemon

salt and freshly ground pepper

oven temperature 200°C/400°F/Gas 6

To prepare

♦ Prick the aubergine and put into the oven for 10 minutes.

♦ Liquidize or crush the oil and garlic.

♦ Scoop out the flesh of the aubergine and gradually mix to a paste either by hand or in the blender or food processor.

♦ Stir in the yoghurt, lemon juice and seasoning and mix well. Serve with crudities.

Serves 4

COTTAGE CHEESE AND WALNUT DIP

Ingredients

⅔ cup/100 g/4 oz cottage cheese

1 tbsp chopped parsley

salt and freshly ground pepper

¼ cup/50 g/2 oz finely chopped walnuts

To prepare

♦ Mix the cottage cheese in a small bowl with the other ingredients. Cream well.

♦ Arrange in a bowl and garnish with a walnut or sprig of parsley. Serve with crudities.

Serves 4–6

Variations

For cottage cheese and peanut dip, blend ¾ cup/100 g/4 oz red peanuts in a blender or food processor. Chop roughly for 10 seconds, add salt, pepper, 2 stalks celery cut into small pieces and ¼ tsp paprika. Mix or, if blending, switch the machine on for a few seconds with the cottage cheese.

SATAY DIP

Ingredients
1 scant cup/75 g/3 oz coconut, desiccated (shredded)
2 cups/450 ml/¾ pt water
1½ cups/250 g/8 oz red skinned peanuts
3 tbsp oil
1 medium onion, peeled
2 cloves garlic, chopped
2 tsp mild curry powder
2 tsp cumin
2 tsp garam masala
2 tbsp tomato purée (paste)
1 tbsp mango chutney
3 tbsp yoghurt

To prepare

♦ Sprinkle the coconut into the water in a saucepan, bring to the boil and allow to simmer for 10 minutes. Allow to cool.

♦ Scatter the peanuts in a roasting pan and put into a hot oven for 20 minutes.

♦ Meanwhile heat the oil in a frying pan over a low heat.

♦ Dice the onion finely and cook in the oil with the garlic for 3 minutes.

♦ Turn up to a medium heat and sprinkle in the curry powder, cumin, and garam masala. Stir well to make a paste, for 2 minutes. Add the tomato purée and stir well. Remove from the heat and add the mango chutney and yoghurt, stir well.

♦ Using a large liquidizer or food processor, spoon in the peanuts and coconut while the machine is running. If using a blender, you may have to prepare in batches. Gradually add the other ingredients until the mixture is roughly chopped. Arrange in a dish with crudities or small crackers.

Makes 300–450 ml/½–¾ pt

HUMMOUS

Ingredients
1 cup/225 g/8 oz chick peas (garbanzos), soaked
2 cloves garlic, crushed
2 tbsp Tahini paste
4 tbsp olive oil
2 tbsp water
juice of 1 lemon
salt and freshly ground pepper
To garnish
12 black olives
4 lemon wedges

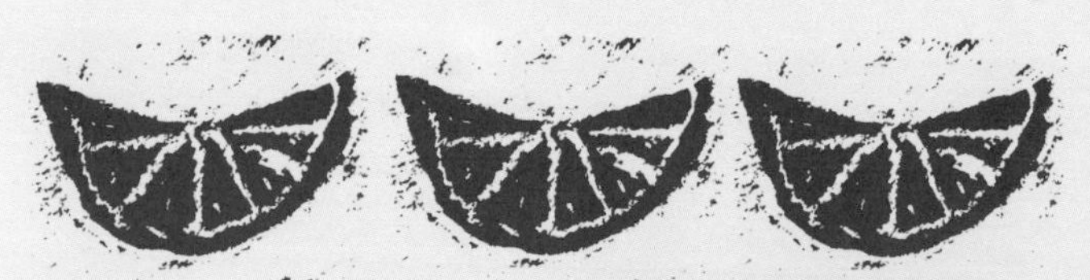

To prepare

♦ Soak the chick peas overnight or for several hours. Drain and place in a large saucepan, cover with cold water and bring to the boil. Cook by simmering for 1 hour or until soft. Drain and allow to cool.

♦ Mash the chick peas in a bowl with a fork and gradually cream in the other ingredients. Add the oil and water a little at a time until the mixture becomes a creamy consistency. Alternatively, gradually feed the ingredients into a blender or food processor until the creamy consistency appears. Taste for seasoning and, if the mixture is too stiff, add a little more oil and water.

♦ Serve in a bowl, garnished with olives and lemon wedges, as an appetizer or snack, with warm, wholewheat, pitta bread.

Note

Canned chick peas can be used if preferred.

Serves 4–6

WHOLEWHEAT SAMOSAS

Ingredients

- 2¼ cups/225 g/8 oz wholewheat flour
- ½ tsp salt
- 4 tbsp oil
- 4 tbsp water

Stuffing

Meat mixture for pasties (see page 78) or vegetable curry mixture (see page 54)

Filling

- 1 tbsp oil
- ½ cup/100 g/4 oz minced (ground) lamb
- 1 potato, peeled, cooked and diced
- 1 tsp mint, chopped
- ¼ tsp coriander
- ¼ tsp curry powder
- salt and freshly ground pepper
- 3 tbsp water
- 2 tbsp peas
- 1 tbsp yoghurt
- oil for deep frying

To prepare

♦ Sprinkle the flour and salt into the bowl and pour the oil over the flour. Rub in with finger tips, as if making short-crust pastry, until the mixture is in crumbs. Gradually add the water and mix to a stiff dough.

♦ Turn on to a floured work surface and knead for a few minutes, until smooth. Put the dough in an oiled poly-thene (plastic) bag and allow to stand for at least 30 minutes.

♦ Any meat or vegetable stuffing of your choice can be used for filling. To make the lamb filling, heat the oil in a frying pan and brown the lamb, separating the minced meat with a spoon or fork.

♦ Add the diced potato, mix with meat, sprinkle with mint, coriander, curry powder and season well. Fry for 2 minutes. Add 3 tbsp water and cook for 5 minutes on a low heat.

♦ Add peas and yoghurt. Allow to cool. Taste for seasoning.

♦ Knead the dough on a floured surface for 2 minutes. Roll into a sausage shape and divide into 8. Put the other pieces of pastry back into the oiled bag while making the samosas.

♦ Flatten into an 18-cm/7-in square, using a rolling pin. Cut into two triangles. Wet the open ends with cold water and seal one side.

♦ Fill the open end with mixture, seal the edge well. Flute the wide edge with the finger tips and press the other two edges with floured fingers to form an even strip. Shape and fill remaining dough as described.

♦ Heat the oil to 190°C/360°F in a deep pan. Fry two or three at a time, turning from time to time. Drain on kitchen paper (paper towels).

Serve hot as an appetizer or as a snack with salad.

These can be made even smaller and used as a cocktail snack.

Makes 16

DOLMADES

Ingredients
1 packet preserved vine leaves (vacuum packed)
2 tbsp vegetable oil
2 large onions, finely chopped
⅔ cup/100 g/4 oz brown rice, cooked
2 tbsp/25 g/1 oz pine nuts, chopped
4 tbsp parsley, freshly chopped
1 tsp mint
2 tbsp currants
salt and freshly ground pepper
1¼ cups/300 ml/½ pt water
¾ cup/175 g/6 oz cooked minced (ground) lamb, optional
⅔ cup/150 ml/¼ pt oil
juice of 2 lemons
oven temperature 170°C/325°F/Gas 3

To prepare

♦ Rinse the vine leaves and blanch in water for 2 minutes, or use according to the instructions on the packet.

♦ Heat the vegetable oil on a low heat and cook the chopped onions for about 3 minutes, until they are translucent.

♦ Add the cooked rice and stir gently. Add the chopped pine nuts, parsley, chopped mint, currants and seasoning.

♦ Gradually stir in 1¼ cups/300 ml/½ pt boiling water, cover and cook for about 10 minutes, until the water is absorbed but rice still has a bite. If using minced lamb, stir in at this stage.

♦ Smooth the leaves on a board and place 1 tsp stuffing in each. Fold the stem end and the sides in and roll firmly.

♦ Line an ovenproof dish with any leaves which are left over. Place a layer of stuffed leaves in the dish, ensuring the seam side is downwards. When one layer is complete, sprinkle with oil and lemon juice.

♦ Continue packing layers until finished, sprinkling each with oil and lemon juice. Depending on size of dish, you may need more oil and lemon juice. Cover with foil and weight with empty baking tins to keep rolls in shape.

♦ Cook for 1 hour and remove from the heat. Allow to cool; excess liquid will be absorbed. Chill before serving.

♦ Place in a serving dish and garnish with lemon wedges.

Extra rolls may be kept in the freezer for future use. They are usually served with a bowl of chilled yoghurt.

Makes approx 60

DOLMADES

Eat vegetables raw whenever possible for the maximum nutritional benefit. Cabbage, carrots, young turnips, cucumbers, lettuce, green beans, onions, spring onions (scallions), mushrooms, mangetout (snow peas), garden peas and radishes are all ideal salad ingredients. Additional fiber can be easily introduced by mixing any of these vegetables with a few cooked dried beans such as haricots (navy beans), butter (lima) or red kidney beans.

Cook potatoes with their skins on — wash them well and remove the eyes. Baked potatoes are always popular and are an integral part of a planned fiber diet. It is wise though to cut out the usual lashings of butter. Filled baked potatoes make an ideal snack.

Boil vegetables in small quantities of water to minimize vitamin and mineral losses. Remember too that the longer vegetables stand waiting to be eaten, the fewer vitamins they retain.

Many beans and seeds are very high in fiber when raw but less so when cooked. It is impossible to eat most of them raw and in the case of some, eg kidney beans, positively harmful. Make sure dried beans have been cooked properly before using in salads.

Use the tables at the beginning of the book to check fiber contents but remember that vegetables' fiber content is diminished by cooking.

BOSTON BAKED BEANS

Ingredients
2 cups/450 g/1 lb haricot (navy) beans
1⅓ cup/225 g/8 oz belly of pork
1 large onion, peeled
2 cloves garlic, crushed
1½ cups/450-g/15-oz can tomatoes
4 tbsp tomato purée (paste)
2 tbsp vinegar
2 tbsp soya sauce
1¼ cups/300 ml/½ pt chicken or beef stock
2 tbsp molasses
salt and freshly ground pepper
1 tsp mustard
oven temperature 150°C/300°F/Gas 2

To prepare

♦ Soak the haricot beans overnight in cold water.

♦ Cut up the pork into small pieces and allow to fry in a pan over a low heat so that some of the fat comes out.

♦ Dice the onion, add to the pork with the garlic and cook for 2 minutes.

♦ Arrange half the pork and onion in the bottom of an ovenproof dish, sprinkle in half the beans. Place the remaining pork and onion mixture on top.

♦ Mix the tomatoes, tomato purée, vinegar and soya sauce with the stock. Mix well. Add the molasses, seasoning and mustard. Make sure all these ingredients are well mixed.

♦ Pour into the dish and add the other half of the beans, making sure they are covered with mixture. If they are not, add some water to cover.

♦ Cook in a low oven, covered, for 6 hours checking after 4 hours to make sure the beans are not drying out. If necessary, add a little hot water as the cooking time progresses and test beans for tenderness.

Note

As these beans keep well, I usually cook double the amount to justify the long cooking time.

Serves 4–6

BAKED MIXED VEGETABLES

Ingredients
2 parsnips, scraped
2 carrots, scraped
2 onions, peeled
2 potatoes, peeled
salt and freshly ground pepper
2 tbsp chopped chives
1¼ cups/300 ml/½ pt milk
1 bouquet garni
1 bay leaf
¼ cup/25 g/1 oz grated cheese
oven temperature 180°C/350°F/Gas 4

To prepare

♦ Slice the vegetables thinly. (This is an ideal dish to prepare using a food processor slicing disc.)

♦ Arrange the vegetables in a buttered ovenproof dish, layer each vegetable and sprinkle each with seasoning and chives.

♦ Infuse the milk with bouquet garni and bay leaf. Bring slowly to the boil and strain on to vegetables.

♦ Sprinkle with grated cheese and bake in the oven for 30–40 minutes.

Serves 4

BRUSSELS SPROUTS WITH HAZELNUTS

Ingredients
450 g/1 lb small Brussels sprouts, fresh or frozen
salt and freshly ground pepper
2½ cups/600 ml/1 pt well-flavoured Cheese sauce (see page 93)
100 g/4 oz hazelnuts, chopped
oven temperature 190°C/375°F/Gas 5

To prepare

♦ Cook Brussels sprouts in boiling salted water for 10 minutes. Drain and season with salt and pepper. Place in a buttered ovenproof dish.

♦ Pour over the cheese sauce. Add the prepared hazelnuts and cook for 2–3 minutes.

♦ Bake in a moderate oven for 10 minutes.

Serves 4

Variation

Use walnuts instead of hazelnuts.

PETITS POIS A LA FRANCAISE

Ingredients

4 tbsp/50 g/2 oz butter

1 lettuce, washed and shredded

12 small button onions, peeled

2 rashers (strips) bacon, chopped, optional

1 tsp flour

2½ cups/600 ml/1 pt salted water

salt and freshly ground pepper

¼ tsp sugar

approx 4 cups/450 g/1 lb shelled peas

3 sprigs parsley

To prepare

♦ Heat the butter in a saucepan, add shredded lettuce (retain some outside leaves to garnish), the button onions and chopped bacon. Cook for 2 minutes. Stir in the flour and season.

♦ Add salted water and the sugar. Bring to the boil, add the peas and parsley. Simmer for 20–30 minutes until peas and onions are tender.

♦ Most of the liquid should be absorbed and the consistency should be creamy. Check seasoning. Serve on outer lettuce leaves.

Serves 4

Variation

Most people use frozen peas. Reduce cooking time to 10 minutes, but cook lettuce, onion and bacon for 10 minutes before adding peas. One chopped onion or 4 spring onions (scallions) can be substituted for the button onions.

Petits pois à la française 43

CORN AND ANCHOVY PIZZA

Ingredients
250 g/8 oz Pizza dough (see page 67)
1 tbsp olive oil
1 clove garlic, crushed
6 tomatoes, skinned and sliced
½ tsp oregano
4 chopped basil leaves
salt and freshly ground pepper
¾ cup/175 g/6 oz cooked corn
8–12 olives, black or green
1 small can anchovy fillets
oven temperature 220°C/450°F/Gas 7

To prepare

♦ Take the 250-g/8-oz portion of dough and roll into a round shape, knead the round out to the 30-cm/12-in size with floured knuckles. Make sure that it is not too thick. (Any leftover dough can be allowed to rise and be cooked as a bread roll.) A large flan tin (pie plate) is ideal for this type of pizza, but it will keep its shape well on a greased baking tray.

♦ Brush over the dough with the olive oil and rub over the whole surface with the well-crushed clove of garlic.

♦ Arrange the tomatoes over the surface and sprinkle with herbs. Fresh parsley may be used if basil is unobtainable. Season well. Sprinkle with corn and arrange olives and anchovies on the top.

♦ Place in a hot oven for 20–25 minutes.

Makes 1 × 30-cm/12-in pizza

POTATO DAUPHINOISE

Ingredients
900 g/2 lb potatoes, peeled
2 onions, peeled
2 tbsp/25 g/1 oz butter
1 clove garlic, crushed
1¼ cups/300 ml/½ pt milk
1 bay leaf
1 bouquet garni
salt and freshly ground pepper
4 tbsp cream
2 tsp fresh parsley, chopped
oven temperature 170°C/325°F/Gas 3

To prepare

♦ Slice the potatoes thinly, use a food processor if available.

♦ Slice the onion thinly. Butter an ovenproof dish and rub garlic over the dish.

♦ Heat the milk with a ring of onion, bay leaf and bouquet garni. Bring to the boil, cover, remove from the heat and allow to infuse for 10–15 minutes.

♦ Arrange the potatoes and onion rings in layers, season each layer.

♦ Add the cream to the cooked milk and strain over the potatoes.

♦ Cook for 1–1½ hours, sprinkle with parsley.

If cooked in a deep flan dish (pie plate), it is often possible to turn out the potato cake.

Serves 4

RED CABBAGE WITH HAM

Ingredients
4 medium size onions, peeled
4 tbsp/50 g/2 oz butter
1 red cabbage, washed and shredded
3 medium size apples, peeled and sliced
2⅔ cups/450 g/1 lb bacon or ham, chopped
salt and freshly ground pepper
3 bay leaves
4 medium size potatoes, peeled and sliced
2½ cups/600 ml/1 pt water
⅔ cup/150 ml/¼ pt vinegar
oven temperature 150°C/300°F/Gas 2

To prepare

♦ Finely chop the onion. Heat half the butter in the casserole and cook the onion for 4 minutes.

♦ Add the shredded cabbage, sliced apple in layers with the chopped ham. Season in layers, add bay leaves until all ingredients are used. Then add a potato layer and finally pour over the water and vinegar.

♦ Dot the remaining butter on the top layer of potatoes and cover with a lid. Cook in a slow oven for 1½ hours.

This all-in-one supper dish can also be reheated and served again.

Serves 4

SPINACH QUICHE

Ingredients
1–1¼ cups/175 g/6 oz wholewheat pastry (see page 66)
Filling
1 cup/450 g/1 lb frozen spinach
salt and freshly ground pepper
1 spring onion (scallion), washed and chopped
2 eggs
4 tbsp cream
1 tbsp milk (for 22.5-cm/9-in flan ring only)
oven temperatures 200°C/400°C/Gas 6 and 180°C/350°F/Gas 4

Spinach quiche

To prepare

♦ Make up the pastry and rest in the refrigerator for 15 minutes.

♦ Line a 20-cm/8-in flan ring (pie plate) (see page 66).

♦ Fill with baking beans on greaseproof (waxed) paper or crumpled foil and bake blind (empty) (see page 66) at the higher temperature for 15 minutes. Remove the beans and allow to cool slightly.

♦ Cook the spinach for a few minutes to thaw. Drain well and squeeze out excess moisture. Arrange in the bottom of the flan ring, sprinkle with seasoning and chopped spring onion (scallion).

♦ Mix the egg and cream with more seasoning and, if using the larger size flan, add 1 tbsp milk. Pour over the spinach and bake at the lower temperature until golden and set. This will take about 20 minutes.

Serve hot or cold with a crisp salad.

Serves 4–6

Variations

LEEK QUICHE

Trim any discoloured leaves from 3 medium leeks. Wash by cutting down the leek and running under the cold tap. Heat 2 tbsp/25 g/1 oz butter in a frying pan and cook the sliced leeks for 4 minutes over a low heat.

Place the leeks in the bottom of the flan case and continue as for Spinach quiche. One tbsp grated cheese may be added to the egg mixture.

MUSHROOM QUICHE

Wash and slice 2½ cups/175 g/6 oz mushrooms. Melt 2 tbsp/25 g/1 oz butter in a pan and cook the mushrooms over a medium heat for 2 minutes. Place in the flan ring, season and continue as for Spinach quiche.

ONION AND PEPPER QUICHE

Peel and slice thinly 2 onions. Seed and cut 1 red or green pepper into rings. Heat 2 tbsp/25 g/1 oz butter in a frying pan and cook the onions and pepper rings for 5 minutes, over a low heat to prevent browning. Arrange on the bottom of the flan ring and finish as for Spinach quiche.

Leek quiche

STUFFED BAKED POTATOES

Ingredients

4 even-sized large potatoes

oven temperature 200°C/400°F/Gas 6

To prepare

♦ Wash and brush the potato skins. Prick with a fork.

♦ Arrange on the oven shelves and bake for 45–60 minutes. Alternatively, boil the potatoes for 15 minutes, drain and then bake in the oven for 25–35 minutes, depending on size. Potatoes can also be baked in a microwave oven – one potato will take 5 minutes but four will need 20 minutes. Crisp in the oven if liked.

♦ Cut the potato lengthwise and scoop out some of the potato, reserve and mix with filling.

♦ Fill the potatoes with fillings to suit individual tastes and reheat for a few minutes in the oven.

Potatoes can be prepared and stuffed and kept in the refrigerator until needed. Heat through before serving.

Serves 4

Baked potato with bean and bacon

Fillings

MIXED CABBAGE COLESLAW (see page 64)

To prepare

♦ Heat the potato and fill with cabbage just before serving.

Serves 4

CHICKEN WITH SWEETCORN (CORN)

Ingredients

1⅓ cups/225 g/8 oz cooked chicken, chopped

1 green pepper, seeded and chopped

1 spring onion (scallion), washed and chopped

4 tbsp corn kernels, cooked

2 tbsp mayonnaise

2 tomatoes, skinned

salt and freshly ground pepper

Chicken and corn stuffed potato

To prepare

♦ Mix all the ingredients, except the tomatoes, in a bowl with the insides of the potatoes.

♦ Arrange in the potatoes. Finish each potato with sliced tomato. Reheat and serve.

Serves 4

TUNA FISH FILLING

Ingredients

1 cup/225-g/8-oz can tuna, drained
2 tbsp tomato ketchup
2 tbsp mayonnaise (see page 58)
2 tomatoes, skinned and chopped
1 spring onion (scallion), washed and sliced
salt and freshly ground pepper

To garnish

2 mushrooms, sliced
2 tbsp/25 g/1 oz butter

To prepare

♦ Mix all the ingredients together in a bowl with the insides of the potatoes.

♦ Refill the potatoes. Arrange the mushroom slices on top and dot with butter and heat through.

Serves 4

CHILI FILLING

Ingredients

½ quantity Chili con carne (see page 72) or
½ quantity Vegetable chili (see page 56)

To prepare

♦ Mix with the insides of the potatoes and refill the shells.

♦ Heat through and serve with green salad.

Serves 4

COTTAGE CHEESE AND WALNUTS

Ingredients

Cottage cheese and walnut dip (see page 31)
1 tbsp fresh chives, snipped

To prepare

♦ Mix the cottage cheese mixture with the chives and the potato filling.

♦ Refill potatoes and reheat.

Serves 4

BAKED BEANS AND BACON

Ingredients

1 small can baked beans or Boston baked beans (see page 40)
4 slices streaky bacon

To prepare

♦ Mix the beans with the potato filling.

♦ Grill (broil) the bacon until crisp. Break into small pieces.

♦ Fill the potatoes with the bean mixture, arrange crispy bacon on top. Reheat.

Serves 4

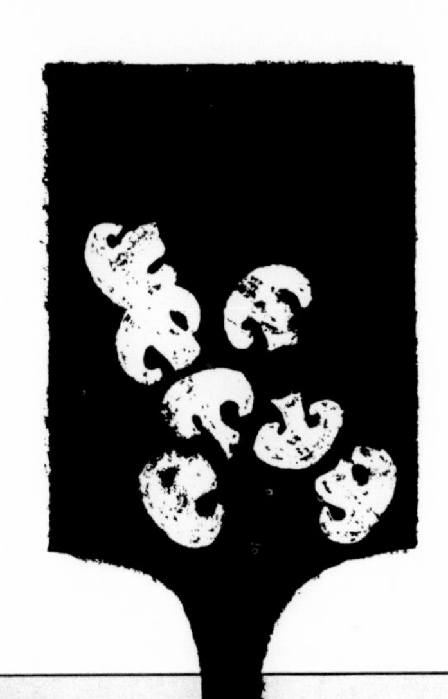

TOMATO SAUCE (POMODORO)

Ingredients

1 onion, peeled and finely chopped

2 cloves garlic, crushed

1 carrot, scraped and grated

2 tbsp freshly chopped parsley

1 tbsp freshly chopped basil

1 bay leaf

4½ cups/1½ kg/3 lb large tomatoes, skinned and chopped

To prepare

♦ Place all the ingredients in a thick saucepan and simmer for 20 minutes until the tomatoes are puréed.

♦ Sieve the sauce or pass through an electric blender or food processor. Taste for seasoning and adjust.

This fresh tomato sauce is really best made with large ripe beef tomatoes and fresh basil. The taste with fresh pasta is delicious.

Serves 4

TOMATO SAUCE

Ingredients

- 2 tbsp oil
- 1 large onion, peeled and diced
- 1–2 cloves garlic, peeled and crushed
- 2 stalks celery, washed
- 1 carrot, scraped and grated
- 1½ cups/450-g/15-oz can tomatoes
- 1½ cups/500 g/1 lb tomatoes, skinned and chopped
- 1 bouquet garni
- 1 bay leaf
- 1 tbsp fresh basil, chopped or 1 tsp dried basil
- 1 parsley stalk
- ½ tsp sugar
- 1¼ cups/300 ml/½ pt chicken or beef stock
- 2 tbsp white wine
- salt and freshly ground pepper

To prepare

♦ Heat the oil in a saucepan and cook the onions over a low heat for 5 minutes until transparent. Add crushed garlic to the onions.

♦ Remove the strings from the celery stalks with a sharp knife and chop into small pieces, add to the onion.

♦ Add all other ingredients, bring to the boil, lower the heat and simmer for 40 minutes.

♦ Remove bouquet garni, bay leaf and parsley stalk and serve with wholewheat pasta.

For a smooth sauce, pass through a sieve or blender or food processor.

Makes approximately 2½ cups/600 ml/1 pt

VEGETABLE CURRY

Ingredients

1 large onion, peeled
1 clove garlic, crushed
2.5 cm/1 in fresh ginger
1 level tbsp mild curry powder
½ tsp ground cumin
¾ cup/200 g/7 oz canned tomatoes, chopped
2 carrots, scraped
1 potato, peeled
1 small cauliflower
2 tbsp oil
1 red or green pepper, seeded and diced
1 tbsp lemon juice
1 tsp salt
1 bay leaf
1¾ cups/100 g/4 oz mushrooms, washed

To prepare

♦ Chop half the onion into rings and use remaining half for curry paste.

♦ Make a paste with the remaining half of the onion in a liquidizer with the garlic, root ginger and curry powder and cumin mixed with 2 tbsp tomato juice, taken from the can of tomatoes.

♦ Cut the carrot into rings, dice potato and bring both to the boil in a little salted water for 5 minutes. Drain and retain vegetable water.

♦ Cut the cauliflower into florets (floweretts) and steep in cold water.

♦ Heat the oil and fry the onion rings for 3 minutes, remove to another saucepan.

♦ Fry the curry paste until brown on a fairly high heat. Rinse pan into the onion saucepan with remaining juice of the tomatoes and 1¼ cups/300 ml/½ pt vegetable water.

♦ Add carrots, potato, diced red or green pepper, cauliflower florets (floweretts), lemon juice, salt, bay leaf and chopped tomatoes.

♦ Bring to the boil and simmer for 25 minutes stirring well to mix the ingredients. Stir from time to time to avoid sticking. Add mushrooms and allow to simmer for a further 5 minutes. Remove bay leaf and taste for seasoning.

Serves 4

VEGETABLE LASAGNE

Ingredients
4 tbsp oil
1 aubergine (eggplant), sliced
1 red pepper, seeded and sliced
1 courgette (zucchini), sliced
2 cups/100 g/4 oz mushrooms, sliced
½ cup/100 g/4 oz aduki (azuki) beans, soaked
2 cups/450 ml/¾ pt Tomato sauce (see page 53)
salt and freshly ground pepper
2½ cups/600 ml/1 pt Bechamel sauce (see page 93)
9 sheets wholewheat lasagne
2 tbsp brown breadcrumbs
2 tbsp Parmesan cheese
oven temperature 180°C/350°F/Gas 4

To prepare

♦ Heat the oil and fry the vegetables in three batches over a low heat, filling the pan and turning in the oil for about 3 minutes in each batch. You will need to allow 20 minutes for preparing and frying the vegetables.

♦ Cook the aduki beans, which have been soaked for several hours, for about 30 minutes until tender, drain.

♦ Start with the tomato sauce and one-third of the cooked aduki beans and the vegetables. Season well. Top with bechamel sauce and lasagne. Season and continue for three layers of lasagne. Top with tomato sauce, bechamel, breadcrumbs and cheese.

♦ When all the ingredients are used, bake until golden brown in the oven for 25 minutes.

Serves 4

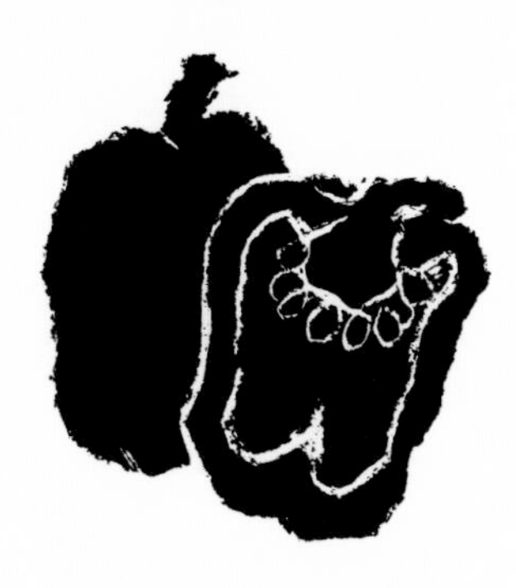

Vegetable curry

VEGETABLE CHILI

Ingredients

2 onions, peeled
1 clove garlic, crushed
1 red pepper, seeded
1 green pepper, seeded
2 courgettes (zucchini), washed
1 small aubergine (eggplant), washed
juice of ½ lemon
1–2 fresh chili peppers, seeded
900 g/2 lb fresh skinned or
1½ cups/450-g/15-oz can peeled tomatoes
6 tbsp oil
1 tbsp flour
½–1 tsp chili powder
1 bay leaf
½ tsp oregano
½ tsp thyme
salt and freshly ground pepper
1½ cups/225 g/8 oz cooked or canned kidney beans
1 tbsp tomato purée (paste)
1 tbsp chopped parsley

To prepare

♦ Cut the onions in thin rings and sprinkle with crushed garlic.

♦ Cut the peppers into rings or dice.

♦ Slice the courgettes and aubergine into rings and spread on a tray, sprinkled with salt and lemon juice. Allow to stand for 20 minutes and then dry them on kitchen paper (paper towels).

♦ Cut the chilis into fine rings and slice the tomatoes.

♦ Heat the oil in a large pan or flameproof casserole on a low heat. Add the onions and garlic and cook for 4 minutes. Gradually add the remaining vegetables, the peppers first followed by the courgettes and aubergine. Add the chili and stir well. Sprinkle with the flour mixed with chili powder, and stir into the mixture. Season well.

♦ Finally add the tomatoes — using fresh tomatoes, ⅔–1¼ cups/150–300 ml/¼–½ pt stock, water or a mixture of both with wine may be added — and herbs. Cook for 20 minutes, then add the kidney beans and tomato purée. Continue cooking for a further 10–15 minutes.

To serve

Taste for seasoning and sprinkle with chopped parsley. This dish can be accompanied by soft Tortillas (see page 126).

Serves 4–6

Variations

50 g/2 oz carrots cooked for 7 minutes and diced or 100 g/4 oz potatoes cooked for 10 minutes and diced or 1 cup/100 g/4 oz peas or green beans can be added at step 6 above after the tomatoes.

WINTER PESTO

Ingredients

½ cup/50 g/2 oz fresh parsley
2 cloves garlic
⅓ cup/50 g/2 oz pine kernels
⅓ cup/50 g/2 oz Parmesan cheese
salt and freshly ground pepper
⅔ cup/150 ml/¼ pt olive oil
2 tsp dried basil

To prepare

♦ Chop the parsley in the blender or with a sharp knife, if making by hand.

♦ Add the garlic to the blender and process for a few seconds. Gradually add the other ingredients through the top of the machine while it is running. When the mixture is puréed, add the olive oil a little at a time.

♦ Add the dried basil when half the oil has been added. Continue adding oil until a thick creamy mixture is made.

Serve with cooked wholewheat pasta.

Makes approximately 1¼ cups/300 ml/½ pt

FRENCH DRESSING

Ingredients

3 tbsp wine vinegar
1 tbsp lemon juice
salt and freshly ground pepper
pinch of dry mustard, optional
12 tbsp oil

To prepare

♦ Put all ingredients in a clean, dry, screw-top jar and shake vigorously for about ½ minute to blend well.

♦ Taste for seasoning and shake again before use. Do not store for more than a few days as dressing is best when fresh.

As salad vegetables are so expensive, serve dressing separately and allow guests to dress their own. This also means left-over salad can be used again.

Makes approximately 1¼ cups/300 ml/½ pt

Variation

To make a herb dressing, add 1–2 tbsp chopped parsley, chives, tarragon or basil to the dressing and shake well.

MAYONNAISE

Ingredients

2 egg yolks
1¼ cups/300 ml/½ pt olive oil
½ tsp salt
pinch white pepper
pinch dried mustard
1 tbsp wine vinegar or 1 tbsp lemon juice

To prepare

♦ Make sure the eggs are used at room temperature and not taken directly from the refrigerator. Warm a clean dry bowl slightly, add the egg yolks, mix for a few seconds.

♦ Gradually add the oil, drop by drop to begin with. Mix briskly with a wooden spoon or small wire whisk. The mixture will become a thick creamy emulsion as the drops of oil are added.

♦ When the mixture has thickened, add the seasoning with a few drops of vinegar or lemon juice. Beat well. The mayonnaise can be made thicker or thinner, according to the amount of vinegar or lemon juice used. Taste for seasoning before using.

Note

To mix with pasta, a little more lemon juice may be used as a thinner sauce is better for coating the cooked pasta.

Makes 1¼ cups/300 ml/½ pt

BLENDER MAYONNAISE

Ingredients

1 whole egg

¼ tsp dried mustard

salt and freshly ground pepper

1 tbsp lemon juice or vinegar

1¼ cups/225 ml/scant ½ pt salad or olive oil

To prepare

♦ Break the egg into the liquidizer, add the mustard and seasoning. Switch on the machine until the egg is foamy, for about 3 seconds.

♦ Add the lemon juice or vinegar and blend for a further 10 seconds.

♦ Turn the switch to high and pour the oil into the centre of the mixture in a continuous very thin stream.

♦ After about half the oil has been added, the sauce will begin to thicken, continue to add oil in a thin stream. If it is too thick, add a little more vinegar or lemon juice, and finally taste for seasoning.

Makes 1¼ cups/300 ml/½ pt

Variations

To make a herb mayonnaise, add 3 tbsp chives, basil, oregano, parsley, tarragon or chervil or a mixture of green herbs to 1¼ cups/300 ml/½ pt.

To make a green mayonnaise, add 2 tbsp sieved or liquidized spinach, 1 tbsp green spring onion (scallion) tops, finely chopped, and 1 tbsp parsley, finely chopped.

YOGHURT DRESSING

Ingredients

1 clove garlic, crushed

½ tsp ground cumin

juice of half a lemon

1 tbsp chopped mint or parsley

salt and freshly ground pepper

3–4 drops Tabasco sauce

1¼ cups/300 ml/½ pt yoghurt

To prepare

♦ Mix all the ingredients together in a jug. Chill and serve as a dressing for salads or vegetables in place of mayonnaise or French dressing.

Makes 1¼ cups/300 ml/½ pt

PEANUT BUTTER

Ingredients

225 g/8 oz peanuts, roasted

6 tbsp oil

pinch of salt

To prepare

♦ Remove the skins from the peanuts by rubbing them roughly between your hands.

♦ Grind the peanuts with the oil and salt in a blender or food processor.

♦ A crunchy butter can be made by running the machine for a few seconds. A smooth butter will take longer to blend.

♦ Store in a jar in the refrigerator.

Makes 1¼ cups/300 ml/½ pt

MIXED BEAN SALAD

Ingredients
½ cup/100 g/4 oz butter (lima) beans
½ cup/100 g/4 oz kidney beans
3 spring onions (scallions), washed
3 small peppers, yellow, green and red
8 slices salami
⅔ cup/150 ml/¼ pt French dressing (see page 58)
2 tbsp chopped parsley
To garnish
2 heads chicory, sliced
2 tomatoes, cut into wedges
¼ cucumber, thinly sliced

To prepare

♦ Soak the butter and kidney beans in separate bowls overnight. Cook in separate saucepans just covered with cold water, bring to the boil and simmer for 30–40 minutes, or until the beans are tender. Allow to cool.

♦ Chop the spring onions. Seed the peppers and cut into thin strips, dice the salami. Place all these ingredients in a bowl with the cold beans and French dressing, mix well. Add the chopped parsley and mix again.

♦ Arrange the sliced chicory around a shallow salad bowl and surround with tomato wedges and cucumber. Pile the bean salad in the centre.

Serves 4

HARICOT (NAVY) BEAN AND COTTAGE CHEESE

Ingredients
1 cup/250 g/8 oz haricot (navy) beans
¼ tsp bicarbonate of soda
⅔ cup/150 ml/¼ pt French dressing (see page 58)
4 spring onions (scallions), washed and sliced
1 green pepper, seeded
1 red pepper, seeded
½ shredded Iceberg lettuce
8 tbsp cottage cheese
To garnish
20 stuffed olives

To prepare

♦ Soak the haricot beans in cold water for at least 8 hours. Drain and pour into a saucepan, cover with cold water, add the bicarbonate of soda and bring to the boil. Simmer for 30 minutes until cooked. Drain and allow to cool in a bowl.

♦ Add the dressing to the cooked beans, then stir in the spring onions.

♦ Cut the peppers into thin strips and mix with the beans.

♦ Arrange the shredded lettuce on a round dish, leaving a decorative ring around the edge. Inside the lettuce ring, arrange a ring of cottage cheese.

♦ Tip the dressed bean salad into the centre of the cottage cheese ring. Garnish with whole stuffed olives. Serve with sliced wholewheat bread.

Serves 4–8

BUTTER (LIMA) BEAN SALAD

Ingredients
1½ cups/225 g/8 oz butter beans, soaked
4 spring onions (scallions), washed
1 clove garlic, crushed
1 red or green pepper, seeded
1¼ cups/300 ml/½ pt mayonnaise or French dressing (see page 58)
salt and freshly ground pepper
Garnish
1 lettuce
12 stuffed olives
2 tbsp chopped parsley

To prepare

♦ Cook the soaked butter beans for about 45 minutes or until tender but not mushy. Drain and allow to cool.

♦ Chop the spring onions finely, add the crushed garlic.

♦ Dice the pepper finely, mix all the ingredients in a bowl with Mayonnaise, French or yoghurt dressing (see pages 58 and 59).

♦ Arrange in a dish lined with lettuce. Garnish with stuffed olives and chopped parsley.

Serves 4–6

Butter bean salad

KIDNEY BEAN SALAD

Ingredients

1½ cups/225 g/8 oz cooked kidney beans

2 spring onions (scallions), washed

⅔ cup/150 ml/¼ pt French dressing (see page 58)

1 tbsp chopped parsley

To prepare

♦ If using canned beans, drain well.

♦ Chop the onions finely and mix with the beans.

♦ Stir in well-shaken French dressing and chopped parsley, chill for 30 minutes and serve as a side salad.

Serves 4

MIXED CABBAGE COLESLAW

Ingredients
½ small red cabbage
½ small white cabbage
6 stalks celery, washed
2 carrots, scraped and grated
2 green apples
2 tbsp lemon juice
1 small onion, peeled
½ cup/50 g/2 oz chopped walnuts
1¼ cups/300 ml/½ pt Mayonnaise or Yoghurt Dressing (see pages 58 and 59)

To prepare

♦ Wash and shred the cabbage finely into a bowl.

♦ Wash the celery and reserve some leaves for decoration. Remove the strings with a potato peeler and chop finely. Add to the cabbage with the grated carrot and mix well.

♦ Wash and dice the apples, sprinkle with lemon juice and add to the cabbage.

♦ Slice the onion finely and add to the cabbage mixture with the walnuts. Mix well with the chosen dressing and arrange in a bowl lined with cabbage leaves. Decorate with celery leaves and serve as part of a salad dish or with wholewheat rolls as a snack meal.

Serves 4–8

MANGETOUT (SNOW PEA) AND CARROT SALAD

Ingredients
3 carrots, scraped and sliced
¼ tsp salt
3 cups/450 g/1 lb mangetout (snow peas)
1 large leek, washed
2 tbsp vegetable oil
salt and freshly ground pepper
2 tbsp chopped parsley
Dressing
⅔ cup/150 ml/¼ pt French dressing (see page 58)

To prepare

♦ Cook the carrots in a small amount of cold water with ¼ tsp salt. Bring to boil simmer for 10 minutes, drain.

♦ Prepare the mangetout peas by removing the small stalks at the end. Cook in a small amount of boiling salted water for 4 minutes, test for tenderness. The peas should be crunchy in texture, drain.

♦ Wash the leek thoroughly and cut a cross through the centre, wash again to make sure all the mud is removed from the inside. Slice thinly.

♦ Heat the oil in a frying pan and cook the leeks over a low heat for 4 minutes. At this stage if you want to serve a hot vegetable salad, add the carrots and mangetout, season well and stir over a low heat. Serve in a heated vegetable dish, sprinkled with chopped parsley.

♦ To use as a salad, allow all the vegetables to cool, mix together, season well and toss in the French dressing. Sprinkle with chopped parsley.

Serves 4

WHOLEWHEAT PASTRY

Ingredients

2¼ cups/250 g/8 oz wholemeal flour

¼ tsp salt

4 tbsp/50 g/2 oz butter or margarine

4 tbsp/50 g/2 oz white fat

7–8 tbsp water

oven temperature 200°C/400°F/Gas 6

To prepare

♦ Tip the flour into a bowl with the salt.

♦ Cut the butter or margarine and white fat into small lumps and mix into the flour.

♦ With the fingertips, rub the fats into the flour until the mixture resembles fine breadcrumbs. Shake the bowl, as this brings the lumps to the surface. Make sure all the lumps have been rubbed in.

♦ Add 5 tbsp water and mix with a spatula. Gradually add remaining water until a soft, but not wet, dough is formed.

♦ Turn on to a floured board, knead lightly for a few minutes. Then put into a plastic bag and rest in the refrigerator for at least 15 minutes.

Use for savoury pies, quiches, flans and fruit pies.

Makes 2¼ cups/250 g/8 oz

Variation

For a richer pastry, add 2 tbsp/25 g/1 oz extra fat and substitute 1 egg yolk for 2 tbsp water.

LINING A FLAN RING (PIE PLATE) WITH PASTRY

♦ Put a flan ring (pie plate) on a baking sheet. If you have trouble with pastry sticking, oil the flan ring slightly first, but, if there is half fat to flour in the pastry recipe, this should not be necessary.

♦ Roll out the pastry in a round shape, giving it a half turn to the right after each rolling to keep the shape. Roll out about 5 cm/2 in larger than the flan ring.

♦ Lift the pastry round the rolling pin and ease gently into the flan ring without breaking or stretching.

♦ Press down into flan ring with the back of the forefinger, again avoid stretching the pastry, otherwise it will shrink while cooking.

♦ Prick the bottom with a fork and neaten the edges of the flan case with a rolling pin to remove excess pastry.

♦ Fill with baking beans, if you wish to bake blind (empty).

BAKING BLIND (AN EMPTY PIE SHELL)

♦ Cut a round of non-stick paper or greased (waxed) greaseproof paper about 5 cm/2 in larger than the flan. Place greased side down in the uncooked pastry case and fill with dried beans, pasta or crusts. This keeps the pastry flat.

♦ Bake the flan case on the second shelf of a pre-heated oven (200°C/400°F/Gas 6) for 15 minutes.

♦ Remove the paper with the beans from the flan ring and finish for a further 10–15 minutes or until golden brown all over.

Note

The baking beans can be stored in a jar and used over and over again.

A 15-cm/6-in flan ring requires approx ¾ cup/100 g/4 oz pastry.
A 20-cm/8-in flan ring requires approx 1–1¼ cups/150 g/6 oz pastry.
A 30-cm/12-in flan ring requires approx 1½ cups/250 g/8 oz pastry.

WHOLEWHEAT PIZZA DOUGH

For a complete wholewheat pizza use recipe on page 67. Half strong (bread) white flour and half wholewheat will give a less solid pizza.

Ingredients

1 tbsp/15 g/½ oz fresh yeast or 3 level tsp dried yeast

⅔ cup/150 ml/¼ pt slightly warmed water

1 tsp sugar

2¼ cups/250 g/8 oz wholewheat flour

2¼ cups/250 g/8 oz strong plain (bread) flour

1 tsp salt

1 tbsp oil

To prepare

♦ To use fresh yeast, cream with 3 tbsp measured liquid in which the sugar has been dissolved. To use dried yeast, take one-third of the measured liquid, which has sugar dissolved in it, and sprinkle the yeast on top. Whisk and allow to stand in a warm room for 10–15 minutes until frothy.

♦ Sprinkle the wholewheat flour into the bowl, sieve the white flour on top and mix well with the salt.

♦ Make a well in the centre of the flour and pour in the oil, cover with flour. Add the yeast mixture and most of the liquid. Mix well until the mixture leaves the side of the bowl, add remaining liquid if mixture is too dry. It is likely that an extra few drops may be needed for the wholewheat mixtures but do not make a wet dough.

♦ Turn on to a floured board and knead well until a smooth elastic dough is made, after about 10 minutes.

♦ Put back into the bowl and cover with clingfilm (plastic wrap) or place the dough in an oiled plastic bag. Allow to rise in a warm kitchen until doubled in size, this will take 45–60 minutes. Knock back (punch down) the dough and shape as required.

Makes 2 × 30-cm/12-in pizzas or 3 × 20-cm/8-in pizzas

PASTA

Ingredients

1 tbsp oil

1 tbsp salt

1–1½ cups/225–325 g/8–12 oz ordinary or wholewheat pasta

2 tbsp/25 g/1 oz butter

freshly ground pepper

grated nutmeg (optional)

To prepare

♦ Use a large saucepan with at least 10–12½ cups/2–3 1/4–5 pt water, add the oil and the salt. Bring to the boil.

♦ Add the pasta slowly or coil long strands until they soften. Stir with a fork to separate and then cook briskly for approximately 12 minutes for spaghetti, or 5–8 minutes for small pasta, depending on the size. It is advisable to read manufacturer's cooking instructions for suggested cooking times.

♦ Test the pasta before draining, it should be firm or *al dente*, that is, neither too hard nor too soft.

♦ Drain through a colander.

♦ Melt the butter in the saucepan, toss the pasta into the butter with a shake of freshly ground pepper and, if liked, some grated nutmeg.

Pasta can then be served with any of the usual sauces such as bolognese, tomato or pesto, or with meat and fish dishes. Pasta served with cheese after being tossed in butter makes a delicious and well-balanced meal on its own.

Serves 4

Fiber comes from cell walls of plants. Although fish, meat and chicken have no fiber they are widely enjoyed and they contain essential amino acids for the growth and repair of body tissue. 'A little of what you like does you good' is the key to these main meals. The critical words being 'a little'. Conflicting information on whether to eat meat or not can be put to one side. The important points are

- *to cut down on animal fats, trim meat and remove as much fat as possible.*
- *use the frying pan as little as possible, and fry with vegetable oil instead of lard or beef dripping.*
- *serve boiled vegetables or salads as often as possible instead of fried or roasted vegetables.*
- *100–150 g/4–6 oz meat daily is excessive. Eat eggs, cheese and butter which also contain animal fats.*
- *fish and chicken, depending on how they are cooked, are less fatty and may be alternated with meat.*

To balance your diet reduce the amount of meat in dishes by adding lentils or dried beans as well as the usual root and other tasty vegetables such as mushrooms, green peppers and peas. Coat fish and chicken with oatmeal, bran or wholewheat breadcrumbs in place of white breadcrumbs or white flour.

Make stuffings with brown bread, oatmeal or brown rice as a base. For variety serve chapatis (see page 124) with curried dishes in place of rice and use wholewheat tortillas (see page 126) to make delicious meals.

SPINACH FISH PIE

Ingredients
1 cup/250 g/8 oz frozen spinach or 700 g/1½ lb fresh spinach
450 g/1 lb filleted white fish
2½ cups/600 ml/1 pt milk
1 bay leaf
4 peppercorns, slightly crushed
Sauce
3 tbsp/40 g/1½ oz butter or margarine
6 tbsp/40 g/1½ oz wholewheat flour
2½ cups/600 ml/1 pt strained fish liquor
Topping
700 g/1½ lb peeled potatoes
4 tbsp milk
1 egg (optional)
salt and freshly ground pepper
2 tbsp oil
1 medium onion
2 cups/100 g/4 oz mushrooms, washed and sliced
2 large tomatoes, skinned
salt and freshly ground pepper
oven temperature 180°C/350°F/Gas 4

To prepare

♦ Cook the frozen spinach in a small amount of boiling water until thawed. Drain and squeeze out excess moisture with the back of a spoon. If using fresh, wash well and remove the larger stalks, cook in a small amount of boiling salted water for 3–4 minutes. Drain and squeeze out excess moisture. Arrange in a buttered ovenproof dish.

♦ Poach the fish in a frying pan in the cold milk with the bay leaf and peppercorns. Bring slowly to almost boiling point and then simmer on a low heat for 8 minutes. Remove the fish to a plate and flake from the skin, remove any remaining bones. Strain the liquid to make the sauce.

♦ Melt the butter in a pan for the sauce, add the flour to make a roux, cook for 1 minute, then add the strained fish liquor, which can be made up to 2½ cups/600 ml/1 pt with water if necessary. Stir over a low heat until there is a smooth sauce.

♦ Place the potatoes in cold salted water, bring to the boil and simmer briskly until cooked. Drain and pass through a wide sieve or mash well with a potato masher. Add the milk and egg and beat to a smooth consistency. Season well.

♦ Heat the oil in a frying pan and cook the onion over a low heat for 3 minutes. Add the sliced mushrooms and stir for a further 2 minutes.

♦ Place the fish on the well-seasoned spinach and pour over a little sauce. Slice the tomatoes and arrange in a ring around the dish. Place the mushrooms and onion mixture in the centre of the tomatoes. Cover with remaining sauce.

♦ Pipe or spread the potato mixture on top and sprinkle with grated cheese. Cook in a moderate oven for 25–30 minutes.

Serves 4

TUNA WHOLEWHEAT ROLLS

Ingredients
4 wholewheat rolls, crusty
2 tbsp/25 g/1 oz butter or margarine
2 spring onions (scallions), washed and sliced
4 mushrooms, washed and sliced
1 small can tuna fish, drained
4 tbsp canned or cooked corn kernels
2 tsp lemon juice
½ tsp paprika
salt and freshly ground pepper
oven temperature 200°C/400°F/Gas 6

To prepare

♦ Cut a round from the top of each roll about 4 cm/1½ in in diameter and scoop out some of the inside.

♦ Melt the butter or margarine in a small frying pan, add the sliced onions and sliced mushrooms. Allow to cook over a low heat for 2 minutes.

♦ Remove from the heat and stir in the remaining ingredients, including the breadcrumbs from the roll. Season to taste.

♦ Stuff the rolls with the filling and replace the lids. Wrap in a square of foil and allow to heat for 10 minutes. Remove from the oven and unwrap the foil.

♦ Serve with a crispy green salad for a snack lunch.

Serves 4

CHILI CON CARNE

Ingredients
1 cup/225 g/8 oz red kidney beans, soaked
3 tbsp oil
2 cups/450 g/1 lb lean minced (ground) beef
2 onions, peeled
1 clove garlic, crushed
1 green pepper (optional)
1 chili pepper (optional)
1 tbsp flour
½–1 tsp chili powder
1½ cups/450-g/15-oz can tomatoes
1 tbsp tomato purée (paste)
salt and freshly ground pepper
1 bay leaf
1 tsp oregano
1¼ cups/300 ml/½ pt stock
oven temperature 180°C/350°F/Gas 4

To prepare

♦ Put the kidney beans in cold water and bring to the boil, simmer for 20 minutes, drain.

♦ Heat 1 tablespoon oil in a large frying pan and over a fairly high heat brown the meat, stirring with a fork or spoon to make sure the meat is separate and free from lumps.

♦ Remove meat to a casserole or pot. Add remaining oil to the pan and, over a low heat, cook the onion and garlic for 4 minutes.

♦ If using, seed the pepper and chili pepper, cut into dice and add to the onion.

♦ Sprinkle the vegetables with flour, stir well for a few minutes, add chili powder and then stir in the tomatoes and purée, season well and finally add the kidney beans.

♦ Pour over the meat, add bay leaf and oregano and finally the stock. Cook for 30 minutes on top of the cooker, simmering until the beans are cooked or cook in the oven for 1 hour.

♦ Serve in Taco shells with salad or in bowls with fresh wholewheat bread.

Serves 4–6

Chilli con carne

LASAGNE AL FORNO

Ingredients
2 cups/450 ml/¾ pt Bolognese sauce (see page 80)
2½ cups/600 ml/1 pt Bechamel sauce (see page 93)
9 sheets precooked wholewheat lasagne
salt and pepper
2 tbsp Parmesan cheese, grated
2 tbsp dried brown breadcrumbs
oven temperature 180°C/350°F/Gas 4

To prepare

♦ Place 4 tbsp bolognese sauce on the bottom of a dish, approximately 25 cm/10 in long × 20 cm/8 in wide. Top with 3 tbsp bechamel sauce and 3 strips of wholewheat lasagne. Season the pasta with salt and pepper.

♦ Start the layers of sauce again: use another 3 tbsp bolognese sauce and 3 tbsp bechamel.

♦ Top with a further 3 strips of lasagne and a further 3 tbsp bolognese sauce and 3 tbsp bechamel. Add remaining strips of lasagne, season and spread the meat sauce on top of the final layer of lasagne.

♦ Spread the bechamel over the surface and sprinkle with grated Parmesan cheese and dried brown breadcrumbs mixed to give a crunchy topping when cooked.

♦ Bake the lasagne for 25 minutes until golden brown. If you prefer a really brown top, the dish can be put under the grill (broiler) until brown and bubbly.

Serves 4

MEAT LOAF WITH BARBECUE SAUCE

Ingredients
2 cups/450 g/1 lb minced (ground) beef
1 cup/225 g/½ lb minced (ground) pork or veal
1½ cups/75 g/3 oz brown breadcrumbs
1 large onion, peeled and finely chopped
salt and freshly ground pepper
1 tsp Worcester sauce
1 tbsp tomato ketchup
1 tsp mixed herbs
3 bay leaves
Filling
3 hard-boiled (hard-cooked) eggs or 20 stuffed olives or 6 mushrooms, washed or 2 medium carrots, cooked
1¼ cups/300 ml/½ pt Barbecue Sauce (see page 93)
oven temperature 180°C/350°F/Gas 4

To prepare

♦ Mix the meat with the brown breadcrumbs and onion, season well, add Worcester sauce, tomato ketchup, mixed herbs and mix well.

♦ Grease a 1-kg/2-lb loaf pan, arrange 3 bay leaves on the bottom. Press half the mixture into the bottom of the pan.

♦ Arrange the hard-boiled eggs or alternately the olives, mushrooms, or whole cooked carrots depending on availability, or use two fillings.

♦ Cover with remaining meat mixture. Pour 4 tbsp barbecue sauce over the top. Stand in a roasting pan with about 2.5 cm/1 in water and cook in a moderate oven for 1 hour or until firm.

♦ Serve hot with vegetables and the remaining sauce served separately.

Serves 6–8

COUNTRY COBBLER

Ingredients
½ cup/100 g/4 oz butter (lima) beans, soaked
2⅔ cups/450 g/1 lb chuck steak
2 tbsp flour
salt and freshly ground pepper
3–4 tbsp oil
2 onions, peeled and sliced
2 carrots, scraped
1 small turnip, peeled
2 leeks, washed
2½ cups/600 ml/1 pt beef stock
1 tbsp tomato purée
½ tsp fresh thyme, chopped, or ¼ tsp dried thyme
1 bouquet garni
1 bay leaf
Scone topping
1 cup+2 tbsp/100 g/4 oz wholewheat self-raising (self-rising) flour
¾ tsp baking powder
pinch salt
1 tsp mixed herbs
¼ tsp mustard
1 tbsp/15 g/½ oz margarine
1 tbsp bran
1 egg
4 tbsp milk
oven temperatures 180°C/350°F/Gas 4 and 220°C/425°F/Gas 7

To prepare

♦ Cook the soaked butter beans in the cold water, bring to the boil and cook for 10 minutes, drain.

♦ Trim the steak and cut into even size cubes, approximately 2.5 cm/1 in in size. Toss the meat in seasoned flour.

♦ Heat the oil in a frying pan over a brisk heat and fry the meat until golden brown on all sides. Remove and place in an ovenproof casserole.

♦ Turn the heat to low and cook the onion for 3 minutes. Meanwhile dice the carrot and turnip. Slice the leeks into 1.75-cm/½-in slices. Add all the vegetables to the onion and toss in the remaining fat. Sprinkle with any flour that is left from the meat.

♦ Add seasoning, stock, tomato purée and thyme. Stir well.

♦ Pour into the casserole, add the butter beans, bouquet garni and bay leaf. Cover and cook in the oven at the lower temperature until the meat is tender, or for 1–1½ hours.

♦ Place the flour, baking powder, salt, mixed herbs and mustard in a bowl. Cut the margarine into small lumps and rub in with the tips of the fingers until the mixture resembles fine breadcrumbs.

♦ Add the bran and mix well. Add the egg and milk gradually and mix well. If the dough is too stiff, continue to add milk until you have a soft consistency.

♦ Turn on to a floured board and shape into an even size round. Cut into four triangles if using a round casserole or eight smaller triangles if using an oblong dish.

♦ Remove casserole from the oven, taste and adjust the seasoning.

♦ Arrange scones on top and put back into the hot oven for 10–15 minutes until scones are risen and well cooked.

Serves 4

MINCED (GROUND) BEEF AND VEGETABLE CRUNCH

Ingredients
2 cups/450 g/1 lb minced (ground) beef, lean
3 tbsp oil
2 onions, peeled and diced
1 clove garlic, crushed
1 aubergine (eggplant), sliced
2 cups/100 g/4 oz mushrooms, washed and sliced
1 carrot, scraped and grated
1 bay leaf
1 bouquet garni
2 tbsp tomato purée (paste)
1¼ cups/300 ml/½ pt stock
salt and freshly ground pepper
Topping
2 tbsp/25 g/1 oz butter
2 tbsp peppered mustard
6 slices brown bread
To garnish
1 tbsp parsley, chopped
oven temperature 180°C/350°F/Gas 4

To prepare

♦ Spread the minced beef in a frying pan over a high heat and turn over with a spoon or fork to brown evenly. Do not allow the meat to lump. Transfer to an ovenproof dish.

♦ Add the oil to the pan and allow the diced onion to cook over a low heat with the garlic for 4 minutes. Remove on to the meat.

♦ You may need to add a little oil to the pan to fry the aubergine on a medium heat until golden brown on each side.

♦ Arrange aubergines on top of the meat.

♦ Add all other ingredients to the pan, bring to the boil and pour over the aubergines and meat.

♦ Cream the butter with the mustard and spread on the crustless bread. Cut into triangles and arrange on the dish, mustard side down.

♦ Bake in the oven for 40 minutes. Garnish with parsley and serve with a crisp green salad.

Serves 4

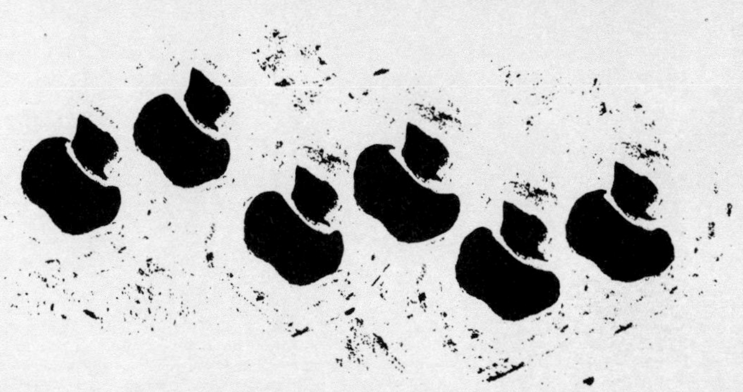

SAVOURY PIES

Ingredients
2¼ cups/225 g/8 oz Wholewheat pastry (see page 66)
Filling
2 tbsp oil 1 cup/225 g/8 oz minced (ground) beef
1 onion, peeled
1 carrot, scraped
1 cup/50 g/2 oz mushrooms, washed
⅔ cup/150 ml/¼ pt stock or water
1 tsp tomato purée (paste)
½ tsp Worcester sauce
salt and freshly ground pepper
beaten egg (optional)
oven temperature 200°C/400°F/Gas 6

To prepare

♦ Make up the pastry and allow to rest in the refrigerator.

♦ Heat the oil in a frying pan and brown the minced beef over a medium heat, stirring to prevent the meat forming lumps.

♦ Dice the onion and add to the meat when brown. Turn the heat to low and continue cooking for a further 2 minutes.

♦ Grate the carrot and add to the meat mixture. Chop the mushrooms and add to the meat mixture.

♦ Mix the stock with the tomato purée, Worcester sauce and seasoning, pour over the meat and allow to simmer for 10 minutes. Allow to cool slightly.

♦ Line 4 individual flan rings (cupcake pans) with loose bottoms or 1 × 20-cm/8-in flan ring (pie plate) with the pastry. (Lining flan rings page 66.) Do not trim the tops of the flans.

♦ Fill with meat mixture. Roll out the remaining pastry in rounds for lids. Roll slightly larger than the ring. Wet the bottom pastry, place on the lid and roll over with the rolling pin to seal. Make three slits to allow steam to escape.

♦ Decorate with scraps of left-over pastry made into leaves or shapes cut with a pastry cutter.

♦ Glaze with a little beaten egg if liked and cook in the oven until golden brown, 25 minutes for the smaller pies and 35 minutes for the flan ring. These can be used for packed lunches and fillings made to suit individual tastes.

Variation

Vegetarian pies may be made by omitting the meat and adding 2 cups/225 g/8 oz chopped mixed vegetables such as potatoes, courgettes (zucchini), aubergines (eggplant), peppers or baked beans.

Makes 4 individual pies or 1 × 20-cm/8-in pie

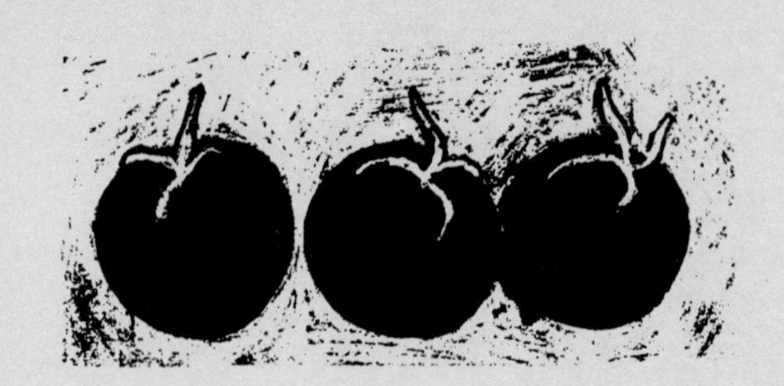

WHOLEWHEAT PASTIES

Ingredients

1½ cups/225 g/8 oz Wholewheat pastry (see page 66)
1 large potato, peeled
2 carrots, scraped and diced
1 onion, peeled and diced
1⅓ cups/225 g/8 oz chuck steak, trimmed
½ tsp Worcester sauce
salt and freshly ground pepper
½ tsp mixed herbs
1¼ cups/300 ml/½ pt beef stock
beaten egg (optional)
oven temperatures 200°C/400°F/Gas 6 and 160°C/325°F/Gas 3

To prepare

♦ Make up the pastry and leave to rest in the refrigerator.

♦ Dice the potato and mix with the diced carrots and chopped onion.

♦ Cut the meat into 1.25-cm/½-in cubes. Put into a saucepan with the Worcester sauce, seasoning, herbs and stock. Turn on a low heat.

♦ Add the vegetables and stir well until the mixture comes to the boil. Lower the heat and simmer for 30 minutes. Allow mixture to cool.

♦ Divide the pastry into two and roll out half at a time to 0.5 cm/⅛ in thick. Cut two 15- to 17-cm/6- to 7-in rounds with a plate or flan ring.

♦ Divide the meat mixture into four and place each portion in the centre of a ring of pastry. Wet the edges with a pastry brush dipped in cold water, fold the pastry rings in half. Crimp the edges and mark three small slits on each side with a sharp knife. If liked, brush with a little beaten egg to glaze.

♦ Cook for 20 minutes at the higher temperature, reduce the oven heat and continue cooking for a further 15 minutes.

Serves 4

Variations

To make vegetable pasties, add 1 chopped green pepper, 2 skinned tomatoes and 1 chopped courgette (zucchini) to the filling, mix with stock or water and simmer vegetables for 10 minutes, allow to cool before filling pastry.

♦ Add ½ tsp curry powder to either meat or vegetable mixture for a spicy flavour.

SPAGHETTI BOLOGNESE

Ingredients
Sauce
1 onion, peeled
2 carrots, scraped
2 stalks celery
6 tomatoes or 1½ cups/450-g/15-oz can tomatoes
4 tbsp oil
2 cloves garlic, peeled and crushed
¾ cup/175 g/6 oz lean minced (ground) beef
⅔ cup/100 g/4 oz chicken livers
1 bouquet garni
1 bay leaf
1 tsp oregano
1 stalk parsley
1¼ cups/300 ml/½ pt stock and red wine
salt and freshly ground pepper
Pasta
225–350 g/8–12 oz wholewheat spaghetti

To prepare

♦ Prepare the vegetables. Cut the onion finely, coarsely grate the carrot. Wash the celery and remove strings with a sharp knife before chopping into very small pieces. Skin and chop the tomatoes.

♦ Heat half the oil in a saucepan and cook the onion and garlic for 3 minutes over a low heat. Add carrot and celery, stir into the oil and allow to cook for a further 3 minutes.

♦ Heat the remaining oil in a frying pan and brown the minced beef over a high heat to obtain a good colour. Turn the heat to medium and add chopped chicken livers. Mix with the meat and cook until brown.

♦ Add the meat to the vegetables with the herbs and wine stock, season well, add the stock and simmer for 45 minutes. Taste for seasoning before serving with freshly cooked Wholewheat pasta (see page 67).

Serves 4

Spaghetti bolognese

BONED HIGHLAND CHICKEN

Ingredients
2-kg/4-lb chicken, boned
Stuffing
6 tbsp/75 g/3 oz butter
1 large onion, peeled
2 stalks celery, washed
1⅓ cups/100 g/4 oz medium oatmeal
1 tbsp chopped parsley
rind of 1 lemon
juice of ½ lemon
4 tbsp stock
freshly ground pepper
butter or vegetable oil
oven temperature 180°C/350°F/Gas 4

To prepare

♦ To bone the chicken, place the chicken, breast side downwards, on the board and split the bird down the back with a very sharp knife.

♦ Ease the skin and flesh from the carcase with the knife and fingers. Insert the knife between the ball and socket of the thigh joint and remove the sinews. Take out the thigh bones, which should come away cleanly.

♦ Hold the joint between the finger and thumb and gradually work the meat from the drumstick. Remove the wing joint from the body and carefully work the flesh from the breastbone without cutting the skin and remove the breastbone completely.

♦ Flatten out the bird on a board ready for stuffing.

♦ To make the stuffing, melt the butter in a saucepan, dice the onion and cook over a low heat for 5 minutes.

♦ Remove strings from celery with a potato peeler, dice finely. Add the celery to onion, cook for a further 3 minutes.

♦ Sprinkle in the oatmeal and stir for a few minutes with the buttery vegetables. Add parsley, lemon rind and juice. Add a little stock until the stuffing holds together.

♦ Lay in the cavity of the chicken, reform the shape and sew up with a trussing needle and thin string.

♦ Rub over the skin of the chicken with the squeezed lemon half, season with pepper, spread with a little butter or paint with vegetable oil and roast in foil for 1 hour 40 minutes. Remove foil for at least 20 minutes.

Serves 6–8

CHICKEN ESCALOPES

Ingredients
4 chicken breasts, boned
salt and freshly ground pepper
4 tbsp bran
¼ tbsp paprika pepper
1 egg, beaten
2 tbsp/25 g/1 oz butter
3 tbsp vegetable oil
To garnish
lemon wedges

To prepare

♦ Cut the chicken breasts in half and place each half between a sheet of foil or clingfilm (plastic wrap) and beat to an escalope shape with a rolling pin. Season each side well.

♦ Mix the bran with the paprika. Dip chicken in beaten egg, and coat evenly with bran.

♦ Heat the butter and oil in a frying pan and, over a medium to high heat, fry chicken breasts on both sides until golden. They will need about 5 minutes each side, turn the heat down after the first 5 minutes. Keep warm in a low oven.

♦ Garnish with lemon wedges

Serves 4

CHICKEN PEANUT CASSEROLE

Ingredients
3 tbsp vegetable oil
2 tbsp/25 g/1 oz butter
2 onions, peeled and diced
1 clove garlic, crushed
2 tbsp flour
salt and freshly ground pepper
¼ tsp paprika
4 chicken thigh portions
4 chicken drumsticks
1¼ cups/300 ml/½ pt chicken stock
2 tbsp Peanut butter
1 bouquet garni
4 tbsp yoghurt
To garnish
½ cup/50 g/2 oz roasted peanuts, chopped
parsley or watercress
oven temperature 180°C/350°F/Gas 4

To prepare

♦ Heat the oil and butter in a frying pan, turn to low heat and cook the onions and garlic for 4 minutes.

♦ Mix the flour with seasoning and paprika and toss the chicken pieces in the flour.

♦ Remove the onion to the casserole and, on a higher heat, brown the chicken pieces evenly. Remove when golden brown, to the casserole dish.

♦ Add any remaining flour to the juices in the pan, mix well and gradually add the stock and peanut butter. Mix and pour over the chicken in the casserole. Add bouquet garni. Cook on top of the cooker (stove) at a slow simmer for 40 minutes or in the oven for 50 minutes.

♦ Arrange the chicken on a heated serving dish. Stir the yoghurt into the sauce and coat the chicken with the sauce.

♦ Sprinkle with chopped peanuts and garnish with parsley or watercress.

Serves 4

CHICKEN SATAY

Ingredients

Marinade

1 spring onion (scallion), washed and chopped
2.5 cm/1 in fresh ginger, grated
grated rind of 1 lemon
¼ tsp ground cinnamon
6 cardamon pods
1 tsp cumin
1 tsp ground coriander
2 tsp peanut butter
1 tbsp chopped parsley
⅔ cup/150 ml/¼ pt coconut milk

Meat and dip

750 g/1½ lb chicken without bone
1¼ cups/300 ml/½ pt Satay dip (see page 32)
spring onion, chopped

To prepare

♦ Make up the marinade by mixing all the ingredients with the coconut milk.

♦ Cut chicken breasts and thighs into small pieces or use a whole chicken if liked. Cut meat from breasts and legs as needed.

♦ Marinade the chicken overnight in the refrigerator or at least for several hours. Remove from marinade and thread on to wooden or metal skewers.

♦ Grill (broil) the chicken skewers for 4 minutes each side under a high heat, then allow to cook for a further 4 minutes each side under a medium heat.

♦ Garnish sauce with chopped spring onion.
Serve with Satay dip and a green salad.

Serves 4

MALAYSIAN CHICKEN

Ingredients
2 spring onions (scallions), washed
2 stalks celery, washed
1 onion, peeled
1 clove garlic
1 red pepper, seeded
1 chili pepper, seeded
4 portions chicken
1 tbsp flour
salt and freshly ground pepper
½ tsp paprika
½ tsp cumin
4 tbsp oil
1 cup/100 g/4 oz toasted coconut
2½ cups/600 ml/1 pt chicken stock
1 cup/100 g/4 oz pineapple, chopped

To garnish
8 strips of blanched pepper
4 pineapple rings
oven temperature 180°C/350°F/Gas 4

To prepare

♦ Prepare the vegetables and purée in a blender or food processor.

♦ Toss the chicken portions in seasoned flour with paprika and cumin added.

♦ Heat the oil in a casserole or frying pan and fry the chicken until golden. Turn the heat to low and add the puréed vegetables. Mix well with the chicken.

♦ Add the coconut, chicken stock, seasoning and pineapple.

♦ Cover and cook for 1 hour.

♦ Garnish with strips of blanched pepper and pineapple rings.

Serves 4

MUNG BEAN AND PASTA SALAD

Ingredients
¾ cup/100 g/4 oz mung beans, cooked
¾ cup/100 g/4 oz wholewheat pasta rings, cooked
4 spring onions (scallions), washed
⅔ cup/100 g/4 oz cooked chicken (optional)
½ cup/100 g/4 oz sweetcorn, cooked
¾ cup/100 g/4 oz cooked prawns (optional)
1¼ cups/300 ml/½ pt Mayonnaise or Yoghurt dressing (see pages 58 and 59)
To garnish
2 chopped spring onions (scallions)
2 tomatoes, sliced
½ lettuce, washed

To prepare

♦ Mix all the ingredients in a bowl with the dressing.

♦ Arrange the tomatoes and lettuce leaves around a bowl. Pile in the salad and garnish with chopped spring onions.

Serves 4

Variation

For a vegetarian salad, omit chicken and prawns. Add 2 cups/100 g/4 oz washed, finely sliced mushrooms.

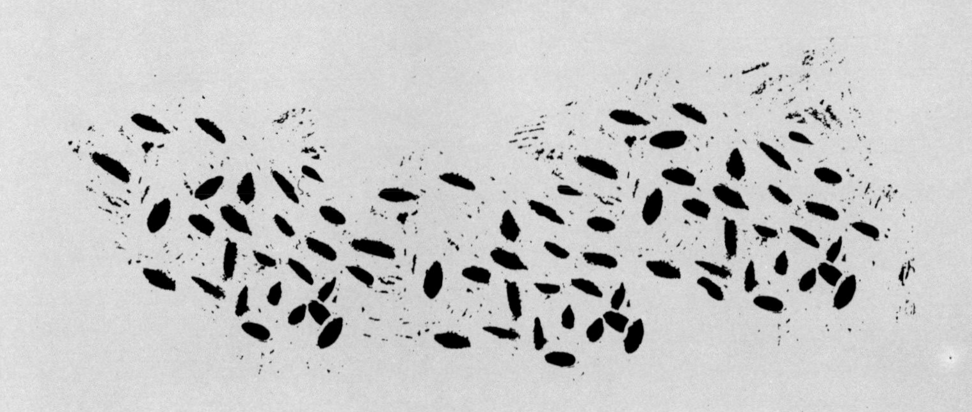

LAMB CHOPS WITH APRICOT MARSALA SAUCE

Ingredients
1½ cups/250 g/8 oz dried apricots
1¼ cups/300 ml/½ pt orange juice
4 tbsp Marsala
2 tbsp/25 g/1 oz butter
1 tbsp oil
4 double lamp chops
1 onion, peeled and finely chopped
1 tbsp flour
1¼ cups/300 ml/½ pt chicken stock
To garnish
Sprigs of fresh parsley
oven temperature 190°C/375°F/Gas 5

To prepare

♦ Cut the apricots in halves and soak in the orange juice and Marsala for at least 4 hours.

♦ Melt the butter and oil on a medium-high heat and brown the chops on each side. Transfer to an ovenproof dish.

♦ Lower the heat and cook the finely chopped onion for 3 minutes. Sprinkle the flour on the onion and stir well with the juices in the pan.

♦ Add the stock gradually and the strained liquid from the apricots. Stir continuously and bring to the boil, season well. Stir in the apricots.

♦ Pour the sauce over the chops and cook in the oven covered with a lid or foil for 45 minutes.

♦ Garnish with parsley sprigs and serve with boiled new potatoes in their skins and peas or French beans.

Serves 4

MOUSSAKA

Ingredients
1 large potato, peeled and sliced
2 aubergines (eggplant)
1 tbsp lemon juice
4 tbsp/2 oz/50 g butter
6 tbsp oil
2 onions, peeled and thinly sliced
450 g/1 lb minced (ground) lamb
salt and freshly ground pepper
2 tomatoes, peeled and sliced
1¼ cups/300 ml/½ pt Bechamel sauce (see page 93)
½ cup/2 oz/50 g cheese, grated
oven temperature 160°C/325°F/Gas 3

To prepare

♦ Drop the potato slices into cold salted water and bring to the boil, cook for 2 minutes and drain.

♦ Slice the aubergines (eggplant) and arrange on a tray, sprinkle with salt and lemon juice. Leave to stand for 15–20 minutes. Drain on kitchen paper (paper towels).

♦ Heat the butter and oil in a frying pan and fry the sliced onion for 4 minutes over a low heat, remove to a plate.

♦ Fry the sliced aubergines on a medium heat until golden brown on each side. Remove from the pan to a plate. This will take several batches, depending on the size of the pan.

♦ Brown the lamb in the remaining oil in the pan over a high heat for a few minutes, stirring to separate the minced (ground) meat.

♦ Take an ovenproof dish and arrange a layer of aubergine on the bottom, top with some of the sliced onions. Spread half the lamb on the onions, season well and cover with half the tomatoes and 2 tbsp bechamel sauce. Cover with aubergine.

♦ Arrange the sliced potatoes, onions and the remainder of the lamb on the next layer, season well. Add the tomatoes and finish with the remaining aubergines.

♦ Top with the bechamel sauce and sprinkle with grated cheese. Cook in the oven for 45 minutes.

Serves 4

Moussaka

PORK AND BEAN CASSEROLE

Ingredients

1 cup/225 g/8 oz red kidney beans, soaked

⅔ cup/100 g/4 oz bacon

1⅓ cups/225 g/8 oz loin or leg of pork

⅔ cup/100 g/4 oz bacon hock

1 tbsp flour

salt and freshly ground pepper

1 large onion, sliced

1½ cups/450-g/15-oz can tomatoes

1 tsp chili powder

½ tsp cumin

1 bay leaf

1 bouquet garni

⅔ cup/150 ml/¼ pt beer

1¼ cups/300 ml/½ pt stock

To garnish

1 tbsp parsley, chopped

oven temperature 180°C/350°F/Gas 4

To prepare

♦ Cook the red kidney beans for 15 minutes in cold water that has been brought to the boil.

♦ Remove the rind from the bacon. Cut into small pieces and cook in a frying pan.

♦ Trim fat and gristle from pork and bacon hock, cut into small cubes, toss in seasoned flour.

♦ Remove bacon to a casserole, fry the pork in the fat left in the pan over a medium heat.

♦ Add sliced onion and cook over a low heat for 3 minutes.

♦ Transfer to the casserole, add all other ingredients including the beans. Cover and cook in the oven for 1½ hours.

♦ Serve sprinkled with chopped parsley.

Serves 4

BARBECUE SAUCE

Ingredients

2 tbsp oil
1 tbsp/15 g/½ oz butter
1 large onion, peeled
1 carrot, scraped and grated
1 green pepper
1 chili pepper
2 stalks celery
1½ cups 450-g/15-oz can tomatoes
2 tbsp tomato purée (paste)
2 tbsp wine vinegar
2½ cups/600 ml/1 pt water
2 tbsp brown sugar or honey
1 tsp Worcester sauce
1 tbsp flour
½ tsp mustard
¼ tsp chili powder
½ tsp mustard
salt and freshly ground pepper

To prepare

♦ Pour the oil and place the butter into a saucepan to heat. Dice the onion, carrot, pepper, chili, celery and tomatoes finely and cook for a few minutes in the oil and butter.

♦ Mix the purée, vinegar, water, sugar and Worcester sauce in a jug.

♦ Sprinkle vegetables with flour to absorb excess fat. Pour on the liquid. Add mustard, chili powder and seasoning and simmer gently for 45 minutes.

Makes 2½ cups/600 ml/1 pt

Variation

If a smooth sauce is required, the vegetables can be roughly chopped and the final result sieved or blended.

BECHAMEL SAUCE

Ingredients

2½ cups/600 ml/1 pt sauce
1 small onion, peeled
1 small carrot, peeled and sliced
1 bay leaf
6 peppercorns, slightly crushed
1 blade of mace
1 stalk parsley
3 tbsp/40 g/1½ oz butter
6 tbsp/40 g/1½ oz wholewheat flour
salt and white pepper

To prepare

♦ Pour milk into a saucepan. Add the onion cut into quarters with 2 slices of carrot, bay leaf, peppercorns, mace and parsley stalk.

♦ Cover and allow to heat on a low heat without boiling for about 10 minutes. Remove from the heat and allow to infuse for a further 10 minutes, covered.

♦ Make a roux (a liaison of butter and flour) by melting the butter in a saucepan. Do not allow the butter to brown. Add the flour and stir well over a medium heat.

♦ Gradually add the strained liquid and stir briskly or whisk until a smooth creamy sauce is made, season to taste.

Makes 2½ cups/600 ml/1 pt sauce

Variation

To make a cheese sauce, add ½ cup/2 oz/50 g grated cheese, ¼ tsp cayenne pepper and ½ tsp dried mustard.

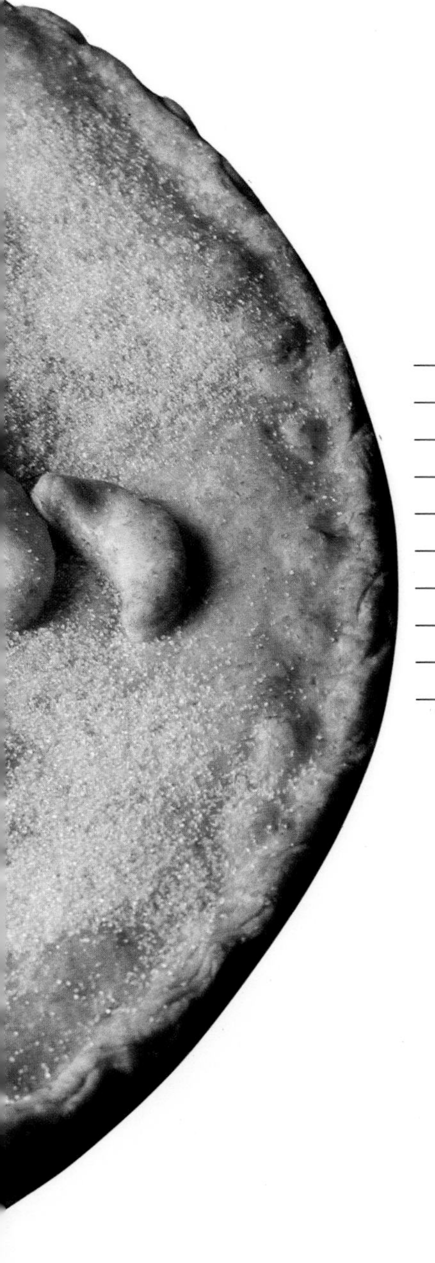

DESSERTS

Desserts are often a favourite part of family meals but it is better to limit the number served in a week as they usually have lots of sugar which is unnecessary in a balanced diet. Serve fresh fruit regularly as dessert.

Wholewheat pastry in pies and oat and muesli topping for fruit crumbles are good sources of fiber. Cut sugar to the minimum if cooking fruit and look out for unsweetened canned fruit. Keep extravagant desserts for weekend treats and special occasions.

CARAMELIZED ORANGES AND STRAWBERRIES

Ingredients
8 oranges
4 tbsp sugar
2½ cups/600 ml/1 pt water
Decoration
8 strawberries

To prepare

♦ Remove the zest from one or two of the oranges with a potato peeler so that you only have the orange zest and no white pith. Cut the zest into fine strips.

♦ Dissolve the sugar in the water in a saucepan. Bring to the boil after it has dissolved slowly. Add the strips of orange peel and simmer gently for 40 minutes.

♦ With a sharp knife remove all the skin from the oranges, peeling around the fruit to ensure that all the white pith is removed and you are left with a complete orange with no white on the outside.

♦ Cut into slices and re-form the orange on a cocktail stick (toothpick). Pour over the syrup and strips of peel. Decorate with fresh strawberries.

Serves 4

BAKED APPLES WITH ALMONDS

Ingredients
4 large cooking apples
2 tbsp sultanas (white raisins)
1 tsp cinnamon
1 tbsp ground almonds
2 tsp lemon juice
1 tbsp syrup
2 tbsp/25 g/1 oz butter
Decoration
4 slices brown bread
4 glacé cherries
24 almond flakes
oven temperature 200°C/400°F/Gas 6

To prepare

♦ Wash the apples and remove the cores, leaving the apples whole. Slit the skins slightly around the equator to prevent splitting when cooking.

♦ Mix the sultanas, cinnamon, ground almonds, lemon juice and syrup together in a bowl.

♦ Stuff into the centres of the apples, top with a knob of butter. Cook in the oven for 40–60 minutes, depending on size.

♦ Toast the brown bread. Arrange on a plate and place each apple on to a square of toast.

♦ Decorate the tops with a glacé cherry and flaked almonds.

The toast soaks up all the delicious juice.

Serves 4

Baked apples with almonds

CRUNCHY APPLE CRUMBLE

Ingredients
4–5/675 g/1½ lb poached apples, sliced
225 g/8 oz crunchy muesli
2 tbsp/25 g/1 oz butter
oven temperature 180°C/350°F/Gas 4

To prepare

♦ Arrange the poached apple slices in the bottom of the pie dish.

♦ Sprinkle a layer of crunchy muesli on top, arrange the remaining apples on top and cover with the muesli.

♦ Dot with butter and bake in the oven for 25 minutes.

Note

To poach the apple slices, peel and core the apples and slice into quarters. Cut into even size slices. Poach in a pan with ⅔ cup/150 ml/¼ pt water, 4 tbsp sugar if the apples are sour, and a few drops of lemon juice.

Serves 4

Crunchy apple crumble

FRUIT CRUMBLE

Ingredients
3 cups/675 g/1½ lb stewed, fresh or poached fruit
1½ cups/175 g/6 oz wholewheat flour
6 tbsp/75 g/3 oz margarine or butter
2 tsp sugar
1 tbsp bran
oven temperature 200°C/400°F/Gas 6

To prepare

♦ Arrange the fruit in the pie dish.

♦ Sprinkle the flour into a bowl, rub the fat into the flour until the mixture resembles fine breadcrumbs.

♦ Add the sugar and bran, mix well.

♦ Sprinkle on top of the fruit and cook in the oven until golden brown, for about 30 minutes.

Serves 4

MARZIPAN DATES

Ingredients
24 fresh dates
4 tbsp/50 g/2 oz Almond paste (see page 123)
6 glacé cherries

To prepare

♦ Cut each date lengthways across the top, remove the stone.

♦ Mould a small piece of almond paste into a thin sausage shape.

♦ Fit into the date and decorate with a glacé cherry.

Makes 24

Marzipan dates

FRUIT PIES

Ingredients

1–1¼ cups/175 g/6 oz Wholewheat pastry (see page 66)
1 kg/2 lb rhubarb, washed
1 cup/225 g/8 oz sugar
3 tbsp water
oven temperature 200°C/400°F/Gas 6

To prepare

♦ Make the pastry and allow to rest in the refrigerator for 15–20 minutes. Cut rhubarb into 2.5-cm/1-in chunks.

♦ Poach the fruit in the sugar and water for 5–10 minutes, depending on rhubarb. Stop when it is sweet to the taste and tender.

♦ Place in a 25-cm/10-in round flan tin (pie plate) pie dish. Roll out the pastry until 2.5 cm/1 in larger than the pie dish. Cut a 1.75-cm/½-in strip of pastry to fit the rim of the pie dish. Wet the rim with cold water, press pastry strip in place. Wet the upper surface of pastry rim, lay on the pie top. Cut the edge at an angle of 45° away from the plate, to avoid shrinkage.

♦ Make three slits for steam to escape and decorate with any leftover pastry, if liked. Knock up the edge of the pie with a knife and flute with the fingers.

♦ Cook until pastry is golden brown or about 25–30 minutes. If liked, sprinkle with sugar.

Serves 4–6

Variations

You will need 4½–5 cups/675–1,000 g/1½–2 lb fruit for a 3¾-cup/900-ml/1½-pt pie dish.

Apricots and apples can be gently poached.

Gooseberries, damsons, blackberries and plums do not usually need cooking. If making pies with fruit that has not been cooked, sprinkle the sugar in the middle of the fruit, not on the top layer beneath the pastry. Cook for 20 minutes at the temperature suggested and then reduce the heat to 160°C/325°F/Gas 3 for a further 15 minutes.

MINCEMEAT

Ingredients
1⅓ cups/225 g/8 oz currants
1⅓ cups/225 g/8 oz seedless raisins
1⅓ cups/225 g/8 oz sultanas (white raisins)
approx 4 cups/550 g/1¼ lb cooking apples, peeled
scant ½ cup/100 g/4 oz glacé cherries, chopped
1 cup/100 g/4 oz mixed peel
1 cup/225 g/8 oz suet, shredded
1 cup/225 g/8 oz brown sugar
½ tsp ground nutmeg
½ tsp cinnamon
½ tsp salt
¼ tsp ground cloves
½ tsp ground ginger
juice and rind of 1 lemon
juice and rind of ½ orange
3 tbsp brandy (optional)
½ cup/50 g/2 oz chopped almonds (optional)

To prepare

♦ Clean the fruit, if necessary. Most fruit is prewashed but, if not, pick out stalks, wash and dry in a warm place for a few hours or wipe dry with kitchen paper (paper towels).

♦ Grate or finely chop the apples into a bowl, add all other ingredients and mix well. The almonds may be omitted, if you prefer a mixture without nuts, but substitute ⅓ cup/ 50 g/2 oz of extra fruit.

♦ Wash and dry jars. To sterilize, place in a low oven to dry. Allow jars to cool. Pack the mincemeat into the jars, cover and allow to stand for at least 3 weeks before using.

Makes 2 kg/4 lb

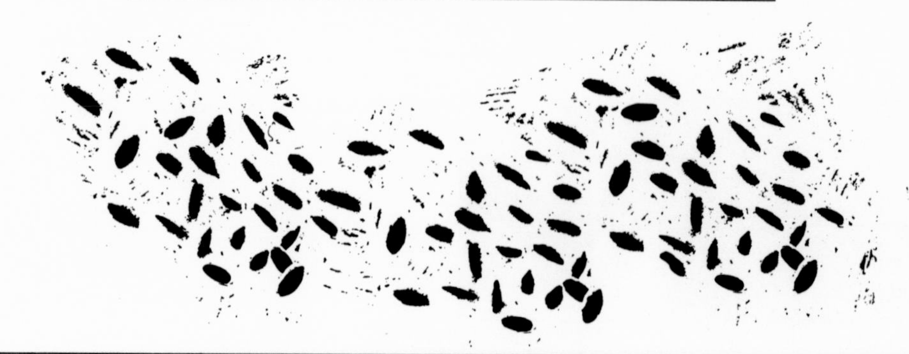

MUESLI, UNCOOKED

Ingredients

2⅔ cups/225 g/8 oz rolled oats

⅔ cup/100 g/4 oz wheat germ

2 tbsp bran

2⅔ cups/225 g/8 oz rolled wheat flakes

¾–1 cup/100 g/4 oz chopped nuts

1 cup/175 g/6 oz dried fruit

To prepare

♦ Mix together and serve with skimmed (skim) milk, milk or yoghurt.

The dried fruit may be chosen from dried figs, apricots, sultanas (white raisins) or raisins.

Serves 8

MUESLI, COOKED

Ingredients

2⅔ cups/225 g/8 oz rolled oats

1⅓ cups/100 g/4 oz wheat flakes

1 cup/50 g/2 oz bran

½ cup/50 g/2 oz desiccated (shredded) coconut

⅓ cup/50 g/2 oz wheat germ

1 cup/100 g/4 oz chopped hazelnuts

⅔ cup/150 ml/¼ pt oil

¾ cup/100 g/4 oz dried apricots, chopped

oven temperature 160°C/325°F/Gas 3

To prepare

♦ Mix all the ingredients, except the apricots, with the oil.

♦ Spread on a roasting pan and bake for about 25 minutes, stirring from time to time. Bake in the centre of the oven, not the top.

♦ Add the apricots when the mixture has cooled. Store in a plastic container.

Serves 8

Variation

To make a mixed breakfast cereal, mix together all bran, bran flakes, bran, dried fruit and nuts. It is as well to experiment with different cereals until you find a mixture that you enjoy.

MINCEMEAT OPEN TART

Ingredients
¾ cup/100 g/4 oz Wholewheat pastry (see page 66)
4–6 tbsp mincemeat
8 glacé cherries
oven temperature 200°C/400°F/Gas 6

To prepare

♦ Make the pastry and allow to rest in the refrigerator before using.

♦ Roll out about 0.75 cm/⅛ in thick to fit a 20-cm/8-in ovenproof plate.

♦ Lift the pastry on to the plate and mould into the sides. Do not stretch. Trim left-over pastry with a sharp knife, cutting at an angle of 45° away from the edge of the plate. If you cut edges angled into the plate, the edge will shrink.

♦ Cut diagonally across the edge of the plate every 2.5 cm/1 in. Fold the pastry back to form a triangle. Remove folded pastry.

♦ Roll remaining pastry to make six even strips.

♦ Spoon in the mincemeat and twist the pastry strips across the tart decoratively. Decorate each square with a halved glacé cherry and bake for 20–25 minutes.

♦ Serve hot with cream or custard as a dessert.

Serves 4

Variation

If serving it cold as a tea-time treat, you may like to decorate it with more cherries after the tart is cold.

Refined sugar has no place in the ideal diet, but tea-time treats are difficult to give up altogether. Try to keep them to a minimum and bake with ingredients that have some fiber such as dried fruit. Use wholewheat flour where possible.
Scones and some pastry can be made with wholewheat flour and have interesting flavours and textures. If the cakes are too heavy for you, begin by using half white flour and half wholewheat flour.
The unleavened breads are ideal accompaniments for curries and spicy dishes, and they are inexpensive and simple to make.
Making your own wholewheat bread is simple and a little bran can be added to supplement the fiber content. If you are not used to baking with wholewheat flour, remember that results will be different from those using refined white flour; follow recipes to start with. Do not sieve the flour or you will remove the valuable roughage.

WHOLEWHEAT BREAD

Ingredients
8¼ cups/850 g/1 lb 14 oz wholewheat flour
1 cup/50 g/2 oz bran
2 tsp salt
2 tsp/25 g/1 oz margarine
2½ cups/600 ml/1 pt warm water (see recipe)
2 tsp/25 g/1 oz fresh yeast or 4 tsp dried yeast
1 tsp sugar
oven temperature 230°C/450°F/Gas 8

To prepare

♦ Sprinkle the flour and bran into a bowl, add the salt, mix well. Rub in margarine.

♦ Warm the flour slightly in a warm cupboard or in the oven for a few minutes. Do not overheat otherwise the yeast will be killed.

♦ Mix one-third hot water with two-thirds cold water and ensure that water temperature is only at blood heat (body temperature).

♦ If using fresh yeast, stir in 1 tbsp water and mix to a cream. Mix with half the water and stir well.

When using dried yeast, add 1 tsp sugar to half the water, sprinkle in the yeast, mix well and allow to stand for 15 minutes until frothy.

♦ Make a well in the centre of the flour and pour in the yeast mixture, rinse out the yeast jug with the remaining half of water. Mix to a soft elastic dough with your hands. After about 4 minutes the dough will bind together and leave the fingers clean.

♦ Turn on to a floured board and knead well for about 6 minutes. The kneading motion is taking one end of the dough and pulling it over the other end. It is a heavy action, which should be tackled with energy. Alternatively, this kneading can be done in an electric mixer or food processor, but follow the manufacturer's instructions for the amount of dough the machine will knead in one batch.

♦ Place the dough in an oiled polythene (plastic) bag and allow to double in size.

♦ Turn on to a floured board and knock back (punch down) the dough with the hands and knead for a further 5 minutes.

♦ Shape the round loaves by dividing the dough into two pieces. Shape each round until smooth on the top. Make a deep cross with a sharp knife on top of each. Allow to rise again for 40 minutes.

WHOLEWHEAT BREAD

♦ Shape the dough into a long strip and roll up. Pinch the ends together and put into loaf tins. Allow to rise and then bake for 35–40 minutes or until the loaf sounds hollow when tapped.

♦ To make brown rolls, divide the bread dough into thirty pieces. Shape into small rounds, place on a greased baking sheet and cover with oiled clingfilm (plastic wrap) or a large plastic bag.

Allow to rise until doubled in size — this will take about 30 minutes. Brush over with water and sprinkle with bran. Bake at the same temperature as bread for 20 minutes.

Note

Place a tray with hot water in the bottom of the oven when cooking yeast mixtures.

To make only 8 rolls, use 1½ cups/250 g/8 oz bread dough.

Makes 2 × 20-cm/8-in round loaves or 1 × 1-kg/2-lb loaf or 2 × 450-g/1-lb loaves or 30 rolls

PINWHEEL SANDWICHES

Ingredients
Wholewheat bread
4 tbsp/50 g/2 oz soft butter or margarine
1 tbsp tomato ketchup
2 hard-boiled (hard-cooked) eggs, sieved
1 tomato, skinned and chopped
24 stuffed olives

To prepare

♦ Cut 6 slices of bread the length of the loaf – the opposite way to normal slicing. Remove the crusts from the bread and roll the bread thinly with a rolling pin.

♦ Mix the butter with the other ingredients except the olives and make a creamy mixture.

♦ Spread the slices of bread with the mixture. Arrange 4 olives along the edge of the slice of bread and roll up like a swiss roll (jelly roll), with the olives in the centre. Place the rolls in clingfilm (plastic wrap) or foil and chill for 10 minutes before slicing into pinwheel sandwiches.

Makes 36 cocktail sandwiches

Variation

Gherkins may be used to fill the centres in place of olives. Peanut butter and cherries make an interesting sandwich for children.

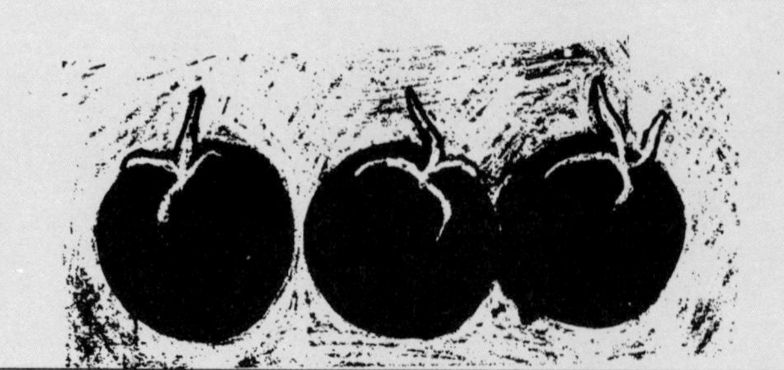

CHEQUERBOARD SANDWICHES

Ingredients
6 slices wholewheat bread
6 slices white bread
6 tbsp/75 g/3 oz butter or soft margarine
2 tbsp chopped parsley or *fines herbes*
1 tsp tomato purée (paste)
To garnish
1 bunch watercress

To prepare

♦ Ensure all the slices of bread are of even thickness.

♦ Make up the butter mix by creaming it with the herbs and tomato purée.

♦ Spread one side of each slice of bread with the butter mix.

♦ Make 2 loaves with 3 slices of white and 3 slices of brown arranged alternately. Press together firmly.

♦ Cut the first 6-slice loaf into 4 equal sandwiches and then cut each section into two making 8 pieces to each slice loaf.

♦ Spread some butter mix on 1 side, lengthwise, of 6 pieces. Reverse 1 section of the bread between 2 sections that have been spread and you will see that a coloured chequerboard effect with the 3 sections stuck together emerges.

♦ Continue making up the sections in threes, spread with butter mix, making sure the white and brown sections are arranged alternately.

♦ Cut the second 6-slice loaf in the same way and add to the loaf by sticking the sections together with the filling. There will be one ribbon left over which can be served as a ribbon sandwich.

♦ Wrap the chequerboard loaf in clingfilm (plastic wrap) or foil and chill for 30 minutes in the refrigerator or 15 minutes in the freezer.

♦ Slice evenly into approximately the same size as a medium slice of bread. Serve garnished with watercress.

Makes 12 sandwiches

Variation

Cream cheese can be added to the butter mix for extra flavour, as can sieved hard-boiled (hard-cooked) egg with a tablespoon of mayonnaise, salt and pepper.

OATCAKES

Ingredients
2⅔ cups/250 g/8 oz medium grain oatmeal
¼ tsp salt
¼ tsp bicarbonate of soda
2 tbsp/25 g/1 oz white cooking fat or dripping
6–7 tbsp water
oven temperature 160°C/325°F/Gas 3

To prepare

♦ Pour the oatmeal into a bowl with the salt and bicarbonate of soda.

♦ If using the griddle to cook, preheat. (If using a non-stick frying pan, it will take less time to heat than the griddle.) Make sure the temperature is right as it is better to work quickly with oatcakes once they are started.

♦ Heat the white fat or dripping. Add to the oatmeal mix and gradually pour in enough hot water to make a stiff dough—the water must be added gradually so that the dough does not become too sticky.

♦ Turn on to a work surface sprinkled with oatmeal and knead well. Divide the dough into two pieces. Sprinkle the work surface with oatmeal again and make each piece into a neat round, roll out to approximately 0.75 cm/¼ in thick. Make an even shape by cutting round a 20-cm/8-in sandwich cake pan or plate. Cut into four or eight triangles.

♦ Cook over a medium heat for about 3–4 minutes or until the edge of the oatcake begins to curl. Remove and rub the smooth side with more oatmeal.

♦ Reheat in a moderate oven for a few minutes before serving. If serving straight away, oatcakes can be placed under the grill (broiler) for a few minutes to become golden. However, if using the grill, do take care otherwise the oatcakes will burn easily.

♦ Alternatively, cut the oatcakes in rounds with a pastry cutter and cook on the griddle or in the oven for about 30 minutes. Allow to cool on a wire tray and store in an airtight container.

♦ Oatcakes are excellent for breakfast served with marmalade or with cheese as a snack.

Makes 16 oatcakes

WHOLEWHEAT AND BRAN SCONES

Ingredients
2 cups/200 g/7 oz wholewheat self-raising (self-rising) flour
1½ tsp baking powder
pinch salt
2 tbsp/25 g/1 oz margarine
2 tbsp bran
12 tbsp milk
oven temperature 220°C/425°F/Gas 7

To prepare

♦ Place the flour, baking powder and salt in a bowl, cut the margarine into small lumps and rub in with the tips of the fingers until the mixture resembles fine breadcrumbs.

♦ Add the bran and mix well, add milk gradually and mix. If the dough is too stiff, continue to add milk until you have a soft consistency (wholewheat flour and bran absorb more liquid than white flour).

♦ Flour the board or work surface with wholewheat flour and roll out the dough to 1.5 cm/½ in thickness and cut with a 5-cm/2-in cutter. Place on a greased baking tray and paint with a little milk and sprinkle with bran. Cook near the top of a preheated hot oven for 10 minutes.

Makes 8

BANANA AND APRICOT LOAF

Ingredients
4 ripe bananas
½ cup/125 g/4 oz soft margarine
¾ cup/175 g/6 oz soft brown sugar
2 tbsp/25 g/1 oz glacé cherries
⅔ cup/50 g/2 oz apricots, presoaked
¼ cup/25 g/1 oz walnuts
2 large eggs, beaten
2¼ cups/225 g/8 oz self-raising (self-rising) wholemeal flour
1 tsp baking powder
½ tsp cinnamon
oven temperature 160°C/325°F/Gas 3

To prepare

♦ Mash the bananas with a fork, add the soft margarine and brown sugar and beat together for 2–3 minutes.

♦ Chop the cherries, apricots and walnuts. Add to the banana mixture with the eggs.

♦ Sprinkle in the flour, baking powder and cinnamon and beat all ingredients together for a further 2 minutes.

♦ Turn the mixture into a well-greased 1-kg/2-lb loaf pan and bake in the centre of the oven for 1–1¼ hours. Allow to stand in the pan for 5 minutes, then turn out on to a wire tray.

♦ Allow to cool, wrap in foil or clingfilm (plastic wrap) and store in a container.

This loaf keeps well and may be served in slices plain or with butter.

Variation

This loaf is also excellent with the following Cream cheese icing.

CREAM CHEESE ICING

Ingredients
2 tbsp/25 g/1 oz soft margarine or butter
⅓ cup/50 g/2 oz cream cheese
¾ cup/125 g/4 oz icing sugar, sieved
1 tsp rum, orange or lemon juice

To prepare

♦ Cream the butter or margarine together with the cheese and gradually add the sieved icing sugar.

♦ Cream until a spreading consistency is reached. Add the rum, orange or lemon juice.

♦ Use to decorate the top of a banana and apricot loaf.

For 1 × 1-kg/2-lb loaf

FAMILY FRUIT CAKE

Ingredients
½ cup/100 g/4 oz soft margarine
½ cup/100 g/4 oz soft brown sugar
3 eggs, beaten
1½ cups/175 g/6 oz wholewheat flour
1 tsp mixed spice
3 level tsp baking powder
¾ cup/100 g/4 oz dried presoaked apricots, chopped
1⅓ cups/250 g/8 oz mixed dried fruit
Decoration
2 tbsp apricot jam, sieved
12 apricots, presoaked
12 glacé cherries
oven temperature 160°C/325°F/Gas 3

To prepare

♦ Grease and line a 20-cm/8-in cake pan with oiled greaseproof (waxed) or non-stick paper.

♦ Mix the margarine and brown sugar in a large bowl, cream slightly.

♦ Add some of the beaten egg, then add the wholewheat flour, mixed spice and baking powder. Beat well for about 1 minute, add remaining egg. Add the apricots and mixed dried fruit and beat together. If the mixture seems too stiff because of the wholewheat flour, add 1 tbsp warm water until a dropping consistency is reached. The cake should be mixed for about 5 minutes before being placed in the prepared pan and smoothed with back of a metal spoon.

♦ Cook in the centre of a preheated oven for 1 hour or until, when tested with a skewer, the skewer comes out clean. Allow to stand in the pan for 15 minutes, then turn out on to a wire rack to cool.

♦ This cake can be stored in an airtight container and sliced for use when needed.

♦ Before serving, decorate with apricot jam and arrange the apricots and cherries on top.

Makes 1 × 20-cm/8-in fruit cake

Family fruit cake

CHOCOLATE WHOLEWHEAT CAKE

Ingredients
3/4 cup/150 g/6 oz margarine or butter, at room temperature
3/4 cup/150 g/6 oz sugar
3 large eggs, beaten
1½ cups/150 g/6 oz wholewheat self-raising (self-rising) flour
1 tbsp orange juice
rind of ½ orange
2 tbsp cocoa
1 tsp baking powder
Chocolate icing
6 tbsp/75 g/3 oz butter or margarine
1⅔ cups/225 g/8 oz icing sugar
2 tbsp cocoa
2 tbsp water
1 tbsp orange juice
30 almonds, flaked
oven temperature 180°C/350°F/Gas 4

To prepare

♦ Prepare a deep 20-cm/8-in pan as for a sandwich cake.
♦ Cream the fat and sugar together until light and creamy.
♦ Beat in one-quarter of the egg mixture, add a little flour. Add remaining batches of egg with a little more flour if necessary. Add the orange juice and rind.
♦ Sprinkle in the remaining flour, mixed with the sieved cocoa and baking powder. Change to a metal spoon and fold the flour into the mixture.
♦ Scrape mixture into the prepared pan and cook for 40–45 minutes or until it springs back when pressed lightly. Allow to stand for a few minutes, then turn out on to a wire rack.
♦ To decorate, cut in half.
♦ Cream fat, add icing sugar gradually, creaming the mixture carefully.
♦ Mix the cocoa with the water and add orange juice.
♦ Blend the cocoa mixture with the icing until it is creamy and easily spread. Add a few drops of water, if icing is stiff.
♦ Spread on the centre of the cake, sandwich the two halves together. Spread around the sides with a spatula that has been dipped in boiling water and dried.
♦ Decorate the top by spreading chocolate icing using a spatula. If liked, pipe around the edge of the cake and the bottom. Decorate with flaked almonds.

Makes 1 × 20-cm/8-in round cake

COCONUT SPONGE CAKE

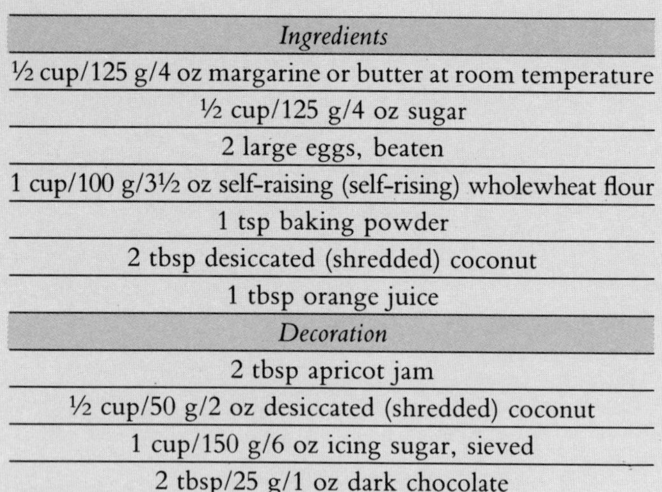

Ingredients
½ cup/125 g/4 oz margarine or butter at room temperature
½ cup/125 g/4 oz sugar
2 large eggs, beaten
1 cup/100 g/3½ oz self-raising (self-rising) wholewheat flour
1 tsp baking powder
2 tbsp desiccated (shredded) coconut
1 tbsp orange juice
Decoration
2 tbsp apricot jam
½ cup/50 g/2 oz desiccated (shredded) coconut
1 cup/150 g/6 oz icing sugar, sieved
2 tbsp/25 g/1 oz dark chocolate
oven temperature 160°C/325°F/Gas 3

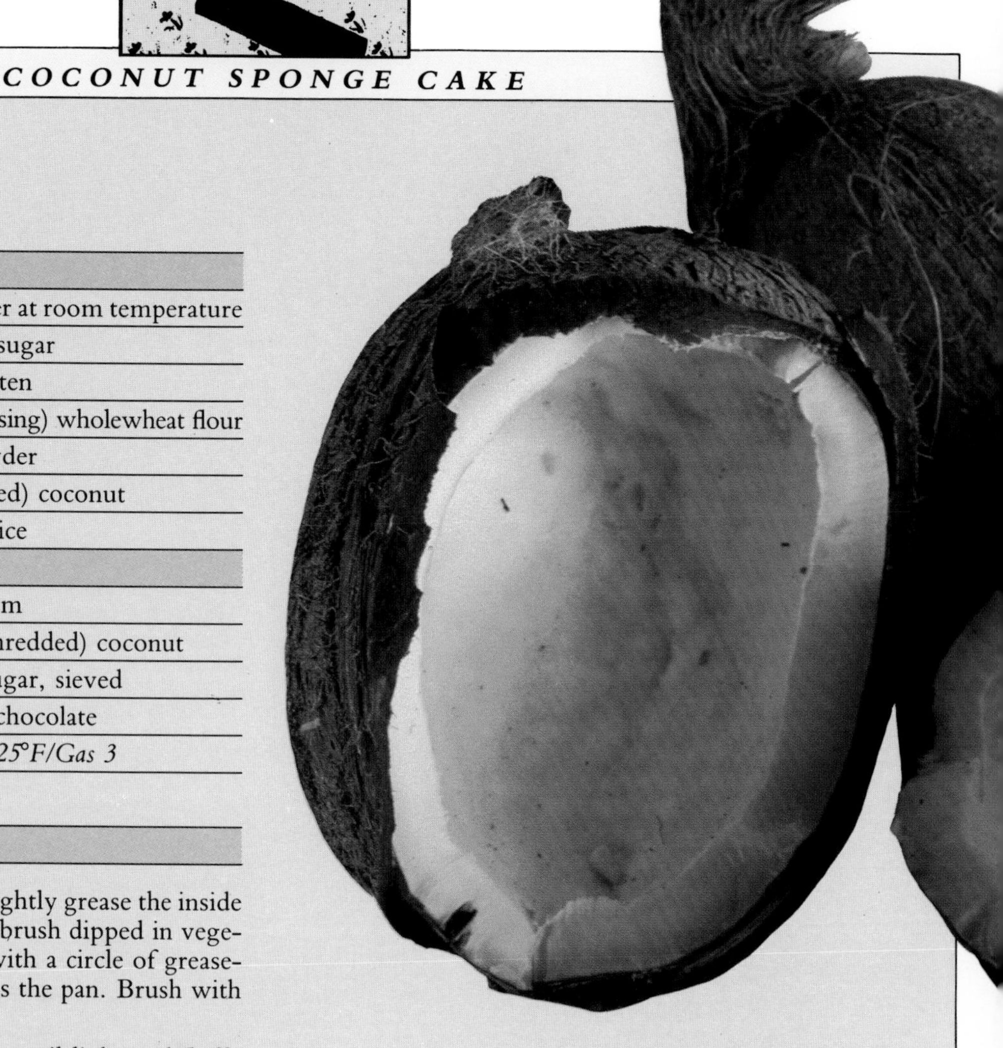

To prepare

♦ To prepare a sandwich cake pan, lightly grease the inside of the pan with a buttered paper or brush dipped in vegetable oil. Line the base of the pan with a circle of greaseproof (waxed) paper the same size as the pan. Brush with oil lightly.

♦ Cream the fat and sugar together until light and fluffy and the mixture falls from the spoon easily when tapped

♦ Add the beaten eggs a little at a time with a little flour between batches of egg.

♦ Fold in the remaining flour and baking powder mixed with the coconut, with a metal spoon. Add the orange juice. If the mixture seems very stiff, add a few drops of warm water.

♦ Bake on the middle shelf of a moderate oven for 35 minutes for a 20-cm/8-in cake or 25 minutes for 16-cm/6-in cakes. Allow to cool for a few minutes, then turn out on to a wire rack and remove paper from the bottom.

♦ Sandwich the cakes together with apricot jam. (If making a 20-cm/8-in cake, cut in half and spread with jam.)

♦ Toast the coconut in the oven, while the cake is cooking, for 15 minutes or under the grill (broiler), if preferred.

♦ Make up the sieved icing sugar with a few drops of boiled water and mix to a smooth white glacé icing.

♦ Spread a little icing around the sides of the cake with a spatula. Pick up the cake with the palms of the hands and roll the sides of the top and bottom in the coconut. Keep turning until the sides are well covered.

♦ Spread the glacé icing on top of the cake. To finish, melt the chocolate over hot water. Make a small icing bag with greaseproof (waxed) paper. Cut a tiny hole in the end, fill with the chocolate. Pipe in lines across the surface of the icing.

♦ Take a skewer that has been dipped in boiling water and dried. Pull the chocolate lines alternately towards and away from you across the cake, for a feathered finish.

Makes 1 × 20-cm/8-in cake or 2 × 16-cm/6-in cakes

MUESLI RAISIN FLAPJACK

Ingredients
½ cup/100 g/4 oz margarine or butter
4 tbsp golden (corn) syrup
⅓ cup/50 g/2 oz raisins
1½–2 cups/6–8 oz/150–250 g muesli (not crunchy)
oven temperature 180°C/350°F/Gas 4

To prepare

♦ Melt the butter or margarine with the syrup in a saucepan over a low heat.

♦ Stir in the raisins and muesli. Mix well. If the mixture is too thin, add more muesli until a stiff, but not dry, mixture is achieved. Pack into a swiss roll (jelly roll) pan.

♦ Bake for 15–20 minutes until firm to the touch.

♦ Allow to cool for 5 minutes and mark it into fingers with a knife. Leave for 15 minutes and remove from the pan.

Store in an airtight container.

Makes 16 fingers

CHOCOLATE CRUNCHY CRISPIES

Ingredients
¾ cup/150 g/6 oz plain or milk chocolate
3 tbsp sultanas (white raisins)
1 tbsp chopped nuts
2 tbsp 'All Bran'
1½ cups/75 g/3 oz 'Bran Flakes'
3 glacé cherries

To prepare

♦ Melt the chocolate in a large bowl over warm water on a low heat. Do not allow the bottom of the bowl to touch the water.

♦ When the chocolate is melted, add the sultanas, chopped nuts and 'All Bran'. Mix well.

♦ Add the 'Bran Flakes' a little at a time and stir until the mixture is completely covered with chocolate. Continue adding until the mixture is stiff and all ingredients are chocolate coated.

♦ Divide with a spoon into twelve paper cases and decorate with ¼ glacé cherry. Allow to harden for about 1 hour.

These crispies can be kept for several weeks in an airtight container.

Makes 12

RICH FRUIT CAKE

Ingredients	*18-cm/7-in round pan*	*20-cm/8-in round pan*	*23-cm/9-in round pan*
	15-cm/6-in square pan	*18-cm/7-in square pan*	*20-cm/8-in square pan*
Butter or margarine	½ cup/100 g/4 oz	125 g/5 oz	200 g/7 oz
Brown sugar, soft	⅔ cup/125 g/5 oz	175 g/6 oz	225 g/8 oz
Black treacle	1 tbsp	1 tbsp	1 tbsp
Eggs, beaten	3 large	4 large	5 large
Wholewheat flour	1½ cups/175 g/6 oz	1¾ cups/200 g/7 oz	2⅓ cups/250 g/8½ oz
Ground almonds	¼ cup/40 g/1½ oz	⅓ cup/50 g/2 oz	½ cup/60 g/2½ oz
Nutmeg	¼ tsp	¼ tsp	½ tsp
Mixed spice	½ tsp	1 tsp	1¼ tsp
Allspice	¼ tsp	¼ tsp	½ tsp
Grated lemon rind	1	1	1
Currants	1¼ cups/200 g/7 oz	1⅓ cups/225 g/8 oz	2 cups/350 g/12 oz
Raisins (seedless)	⅔ cup/100 g/4 oz	¾ cup/125 g/5 oz	1 cup/150 g/6 oz
Sultanas (white raisins)	¾ cup/125 g/5 oz	1 cup/150 g/6 oz	1⅓ cups/250 g/8 oz
Glacé cherries	¼ cup/50 g/2 oz	¼ cup/50 g/2 oz	⅓ cup/75 g/3 oz
Mixed peel	½ cup/50 g/2 oz	¾ cup/75 g/3 oz	1 cup/100 g/4 oz
Chopped almonds	1 tbsp/25 g/1 oz	1 tbsp/25 g/1 oz	1½ tbsp/40 g/1½ oz
Brandy or sherry	1 tbsp	1½ tbsp	2 tbsp
oven temperature 140°C/275°F/Gas 1			

If cooking fruit cakes in a fan-assisted (convection) oven, check the manufacturer's instructions as the cooking time may be slightly less.

To prepare a cake pan for a rich fruit cake

♦ Cut a strip of greaseproof (waxed) 5 cm/2 in wider than the depth of the cake pan for its side. If using greaseproof (waxed) paper, this strip may be doubled. Non-stick paper will be single sheet.

♦ Make a 2.5-cm/1-in strip along the bottom (lengthways), fold a hem and then cut the fold diagonally at 1-cm/½-in intervals.

♦ Oil the inside of the pan and the greaseproof (waxed) paper and arrange it on the inside of the pan with the snipped edge flat on the bottom of the pan.

♦ Cut a double circle of paper the same size as the bottom of the pan, oil and place on top of the cut edges from the side.

♦ Tie a band of brown paper around the outside for extra protection.

Method

♦ Cream the margarine and sugar together in a bowl either by hand or with an electric mixer. The mixture should be light and fluffy and drop easily from a spoon when tapped on the side of the bowl.

♦ When the mixture is creamed, add the treacle and continue creaming for a further 2 minutes. Add some beaten egg and cream well. At this stage, 2 tsp flour can be added before gradually beating in more egg. Add 1 tbsp flour between each addition of egg.

♦ When all the eggs have been added, change to a metal spoon and fold in the remaining flour mixed with the spices and the mixed fruit. Make sure the fruit and nuts are well mixed into the mixture. Add the brandy or sherry.

♦ Empty the cake mixture into the prepared pan and smooth the top with the back of a wet tablespoon. Make a slight indentation in the centre to allow the cake to rise evenly.

♦ Bake in the middle of a low oven for 3 hours and then test the cake every 15 minutes. This should be done by prodding with a skewer, which will come out without any mixture sticking to it when the cake is completely cooked.

♦ Allow to stand for 20 minutes before taking out of the pan and removing the paper. Cool on a wire rack.

This cake will keep well for months in an airtight container.

For special occasions, decorate as instructed on page 123.

ALMOND PASTE

Ingredients

2½ cups/350 g/12 oz ground almonds

1 cup/175 g/6 oz icing sugar

¾ cup/175 g/6 oz sugar

1 medium egg

1 tsp lemon juice

few drops almond essence (extract)

apricot jam, sieved

To prepare

♦ Place the ground almonds, icing sugar and sugar into a mixing bowl. Mix well.

♦ Add all the other ingredients and knead together with fingertips.

♦ To cover a cake (eg Rich Fruit Cake, see page 122), brush the top and sides with warm sieved apricot jam. Dust the work surface with icing sugar and roll out one-third of the almond paste slightly larger than the top of the cake. Place the paste on to the top of the cake and trim away excess.

♦ Cut a strip of greaseproof (waxed) paper to the exact size of the sides of the cake, widthways and lengthways.

♦ Roll the remaining almond paste into a long strip to fit the paper, which can be dusted with icing sugar. Lift the paper and place the marzipan around the cake. Mould edges with fingers dipped in icing sugar.

♦ Allow cake to dry for 3 days before icing.

To cover a 20-cm/8-in cake

FONDANT ICING

Ingredients

2½ cups/350 g/12 oz icing sugar

1–2 tbsp liquid glucose

1 egg white

1 tbsp icing sugar and cornflour

To prepare

♦ Sieve the icing sugar in a bowl. Make a well in the centre, add the liquid glucose and some egg white and mix together with a spatula. When the mixture is well mixed, knead together with the hands until a ball is formed.

♦ Dredge the worktop with icing sugar and work the mixture into a round shape.

♦ Roll out the icing until it is 7 cm/3 in larger than the cake. Brush the almond paste on the cake with a little egg white. Lift the icing on carefully and mould it over the cake with fingers dipped in the icing sugar and cornflour mixture.

♦ Finish round the edges, when hardened, with piped royal icing or moulded flowers.

To cover an 18-cm/7-in round cake

ROYAL ICING

Ingredients

2 egg whites

3⅓ cups/450 g/1 lb icing sugar, sieved

2 drops lemon juice

1 tsp glycerine

To prepare

♦ Place the egg whites in a bowl and whisk until slightly frothy with a fork.

♦ Add icing sugar gradually and beat well with a wooden spoon or electric mixer until the icing is smooth, glossy and thick enough to hold its shape when spread.

♦ Beat in lemon juice and glycerine, allow to stand for 1 hour. Colour may be added at this stage. Cover with a damp cloth.

♦ Secure the cake on a board with a little icing. Pour some icing on top of the cake. Use a metal ruler to draw the icing across the surface smoothly. Allow to stand and dry for 24 hours.

♦ Use the same process on the sides of the cake, using the ruler vertically to remove excess. Allow to dry. Use at least 3 layers of icing for a smooth surface, allowing them to dry between coats.

♦ A smaller amount of slightly stiffer icing can be made up for decoration to suit the occasion.

Florists' ribbons and fresh flowers are always simple and pretty to finish a cake.

To cover a 20-cm/8-in cake

CHAPATIS

Ingredients
1½ cups/175 g/6 oz wholewheat flour
pinch of salt
10 tbsp water

To prepare

♦ Sprinkle the flour into a bowl with the salt. Work in the water gradually with a round-bladed knife to form a soft dough. Do not let the dough become sticky.

♦ Turn on to a floured work surface and knead until smooth. Cover with a damp, clean cloth. Allow to stand for 30 minutes.

♦ Flour the board again, knead the dough for 1 minute, shape it into a roll and cut into 8 pieces. Flour your hands and the work surface and roll each piece into a ball.

♦ Take each ball and flatten it by hand or with light pressure of a rolling pin. When the chapatis are 18 cm/6 in across, finish shaping into rounds and shake off excess flour.

♦ Heat a lightly oiled griddle or frying pan on a high heat. Turn the heat down to low and cook one side and then the other of each chapati for a few seconds. The chapatis will have white spots.

♦ Traditionally each side is now put on to a low flame for a few seconds to puff up. If this seems too daunting, heat the grill (broiler) to high then turn to low and place the chapatis near the heat. This will complete the cooking and make them puff up.

If you are not going to eat them immediately, wrap them in foil, store them in the refrigerator and reheat them, when required, in a very hot oven for 10–15 minutes.

Makes 8

PARATHAS

Ingredients
4¼ cups/450 g/1 lb wholewheat flour
1 tsp salt
2 tbsp oil
1¼ cups/250 ml/scant ½ pt water

To prepare

♦ Add the flour to the salt and gradually add a few drops of oil and the water, mixing all the time with the hands until you have a pliable dough.

♦ Knead the dough well. Then cover it with a damp cloth or place in a damp polythene (plastic) bag. Allow to stand at room temperature for 1 hour.

♦ Make a roll of the dough and cut into six pieces. Roll out each ball until it is a thin circle. Rub over with oil, fold in half then again, into quarters. Roll out again and brush with oil. The parathas should be triangular shape.

♦ Heat the griddle or non-stick frying pan, brush with oil, and fry until golden on each side. After a few seconds, press the edges with a spatula and they will start to puff. Cook until golden and spotted on each side.

Makes 6

STUFFED PARATHAS

Ingredients
Paratha mixture (see page 125)
Filling
approx 3 cups/250 g/8 oz potatoes, peeled and sliced
1 tbsp oil
1 onion, peeled
1 grated carrot
¼ tsp curry powder
juice of ½ lemon
1 tbsp parsley
½ tsp salt

To prepare

♦ Make one quantity of Paratha mixture.

♦ Divide mixture into six balls. Cover with damp cloth and allow to stand at room temperature for 1 hour.

♦ Boil the potatoes until tender, dice but do not mash.

♦ Heat the oil in a frying pan and cook the onion for 4 minutes, add the cooked potato, drained, and the carrot, sprinkle with curry powder and fry for a further 2 minutes. Add lemon juice, parsley and salt. Allow the mixture to cool in the refrigerator.

♦ Roll out each ball into a thin circle. Rub over with oil, fold in half and then again, into quarters. Open one-quarter and put in one-sixth of filling. Seal the edges and roll out into a triangular shape, brush on both sides with oil.

♦ Heat the griddle or non-stick frying pan, brush on both sides with oil, and fry in 2 tbsp oil until golden on each side. After a few seconds, press the edges with a spatula and they will start to puff. Cook until golden brown and spotted on each side.

Makes 6

SOFT TORTILLAS

Ingredients
2¼ cups/250 g/8 oz wholewheat flour
1 tsp baking powder
1 tsp salt
4 tbsp/50 g/2 oz white cooking fat
4 tbsp water

To prepare

♦ Place the flour in a bowl with baking powder and salt. Cut the fat in small lumps and add to the flour.

♦ Add enough water to make a soft dough, starting with 3 tbsp and adding the last part gradually.

♦ Turn the paste on to a lightly floured board and knead for a few seconds until the dough is smooth.

♦ Divide into eight balls and cover with a damp tea towel or clingfilm (plastic wrap). Allow to stand for 15 minutes.

♦ Roll each ball into a 15-cm/6-in round. Cut evenly with a plate or sandwich pan.

♦ Rub a non-stick frying pan or griddle over with oiled kitchen paper (paper towels).

♦ Place each round on the griddle or frying pan and cook until lightly brown on each side.

Store in foil or clingfilm (plastic wrap) in the fridge if not using immediately. Reheat on the griddle or frying pan for a few seconds each side. If reheating in the oven, place on a baking sheet in a hot oven for a few minutes. Do not overcook otherwise the tortillas will become hard.

Makes 8